WORLD OF GRAMMAR AND WRITING

3

T0343850

NATIONAL GEOGRAPHIC

L E A R N I N G

Australia · Brazil · Mexico · Singapore · United Kingdom · United States

Contents

Grammar

Writing

Present simple and present continuous

Present simple

Affirmative	Negative	Question
I/you read	I/you do not (don't) read	Do I/you read?
he/she/it reads	he/she/it does not (doesn't) read	Does he/she/it read?
we/you/they read	we/you/they do not (don't) read	Do we/you/they read?

Short answers	
Yes, I/you do.	No, I/you don't.
Yes, he/she/it does.	No, he/she/it doesn't.
Yes, we/you/they do.	No, we/you/they don't.

We use the present simple to talk about:

- habits.
  *She **sees** her grandparents every week.*
  *He **doesn't cycle** to school.*

- things that are true in general.
  *The sun **sets** in the west.*
  *It **is** often cold in winter.*

- permanent states.
  *We **live** in the UK.*
  *She **has** curly hair.*

Notes

We can use negative questions when we want to show that we are surprised about something. ***Aren't** you cold? You don't have a coat.*

My family always eats outside in the summer. My grandparents are here today too.

1 **Complete the sentences with the present simple.**

1   I _____go_____ (go) to the gym every week.

2   She _____ (not wait) for the bus every morning.

3   They always _____ (eat) vegetables.

4   It _____ (be) cold and wet in winter.

5   My teacher _____ (come) from the USA.

6   We _____ (not see) them very often.

7   The headteacher _____ (sit) in his office all day.

8   My sister only _____ (watch) films on Saturdays.

9   Water _____ (freeze) at zero degrees Celsius.

10 He _____ (do) puzzles at the weekend.

2 **Complete the questions with the present simple.**

1   ____Does she____ always _____ski_____ (she / ski) in the mountains?

2   _____ ever _____ (he / walk) to school?

3   _____ (they / live) in Poland?

4   _____ (we / need) any yoghurts?

5   _____ (they / know) the way to the lake?

6   _____ sometimes _____ (you / practise) the piano?

7   _____ (his parents / help) him with his homework?

8   _____ (the weather / get) very hot in the summer?

9   _____ (he / go) out with his friends every day?

10 _____ (she / play) computer games at home?

Adverbs of frequency with the present simple

never	*rarely*	*sometimes*	*often*	*usually*	*always*
0%					100%

Adverbs of frequency come before the main verb but after the verb *to be*.
He **often** watches TV in the evening.
She is **sometimes** late for school.

3   **Rewrite the sentences with the adverbs of frequency in the correct place.**

1   She goes swimming in the winter. (never)

   She never goes swimming in the winter.

2   They go to the beach. (rarely)

   _____

3   I make my bed. (sometimes)

   _____

4   Are they at home in the evenings? (always)

   _____

5   Does the train leave on time? (usually)

   _____

6   She is late for her classes. (never)

   _____

7   Dad rides on a motorcycle. (sometimes)

   _____

8   Do you have a lot of homework? (often)

   _____

Time expressions with the present simple

every day	in the mornings
every week	in the afternoons
every month	in the evenings
every year	on Mondays
every summer	on Tuesday mornings
every other day	three times a day
every two months	once a week
at the weekend	twice a month
in December	

Time expressions usually come at the end of a sentence. We put them at the beginning of a sentence when we want to emphasise them.

*They go to summer camp **every year**.*

***On Saturday mornings**, we go to the shopping centre.*

---

4   **Write sentences about yourself using the time expressions.**

1   (every summer) _I go on a beach holiday every summer._

2   (at the weekend) _____

3   (in the evenings) _____

4   (every week) _____

5   (once a month) _____

6   (twice a day) _____

7   (in December) _____

8   (every year) _____

Present continuous

Affirmative	Negative	Question
I am (I'm) reading you are (you're) reading he/she/it is (he's/she's/it's) reading we/you/they are (we're/you're/they're) reading	I am not (I'm not) reading you are not (aren't) reading he/she/it is not (isn't) reading we/you/they are not (aren't) reading	Am I reading? Are you reading? Is he/she/it reading? Are we/you/they reading?

Short answers

Yes, I am.	No, I'm not.
Yes, you are.	No, you aren't.
Yes, he/she/it is.	No, he/she/it isn't.
Yes, we/you/they are.	No, we/you/they aren't.

We use the present continuous to talk about:

* actions in progress at the time of speaking.
  *She's **planting** flowers in the garden now.*
  ***Is** he **using** the computer at the moment?*

* actions in progress around the time of speaking.
  *I'm **going** to the theatre with my grandparents this week.*
  *They **are learning** Russian this year.*

Notes

We can use negative questions when we want to show that we are surprised about something.
*Why **aren't** you **eating** your lunch?*

5 **Complete the sentences with the words from the box. Use the present continuous.**

catch	have	not go	not listen	make	~~roller skate~~	not stay	talk	teach	watch

1   The boys _____are roller skating_____ in the park.
2   I _____ the bus to school this morning.
3   He _____ long in Japan, maybe only a week.
4   I think I _____ to the wrong person.
5   She _____ to school today.
6   We _____ the fireworks display. Isn't it wonderful?
7   I _____ a cake for my dad's birthday.
8   My friends _____ a picnic in the park today.
9   They _____ to what he is telling them.
10 Maria _____ her brother about the solar system.

6 **Complete the questions with the present continuous.**

1   _____Is the baby sleeping_____ (the baby / sleep) at the moment?

2   What _____ (you / eat)?

3   _____ (they / travel) from Italy to Spain?

4   _____ (she / cook) pasta for dinner?

5   _____ (you / collect) stamps?

6   Why _____ (he / not do) his homework?

7   _____ (Dana / play) computer games?

8   _____ (they / read) comic books?

9   _____ (the girls / drink) milkshakes?

10   _____ (he / stay) at home tonight?

Think about it!

Questions in the present simple or the present continuous have the same word order when they start with question words (*what, why,* etc.).

Time expressions with the present continuous

at the moment	this afternoon
for the time being	this week
now	this month
right now	this year
this morning	today

---

7 **Complete the sentences with the present simple or the present continuous.**

1   We usually _____have_____ (have) breakfast at seven o'clock.

2   When I _____ (go) on holiday in the summer, I _____ (swim) in the sea every day.

3   The teenagers _____ (listen) to music in their bedroom at the moment.

4   What _____ (you / do) on Saturdays?

5   They _____ (live) in Brazil at the moment because their dad _____ (work) there.

6   I can't talk right now. I _____ (do) the washing up.

7   What _____ usually _____ (you / have) for lunch?

8   What language _____ (you / speak)? Is it Spanish?

Stative verbs

We don't usually use stative verbs in the present continuous. Stative verbs are:

- verbs of senses.
  feel, hear, see, smell, sound, taste
  The biscuits **taste** delicious!

- verbs of feeling.
  dislike, hate, like, love, need, prefer, want
  He **doesn't like** going snowboarding.

- verbs of understanding.
  appear, believe, forget, hope, imagine, know, mean, remember, seem, think, understand
  She **seems** to be very calm.

- verbs of possession.
  belong to, own
  That coat **belongs** to my sister.

We can use some stative verbs in the present continuous, but there is a change in meaning.

When we use the verb *see* in the present continuous, it means *meet* or *visit*.
I**'m seeing** my friends on Friday.

The verb *think* usually means *have the opinion* or *believe*.
I **think** these pancakes are wonderful.

When we use the verb *think* in the present continuous, it means *use the mind*.
Please be quiet! I**'m thinking**.

Notes

We often use the verbs of senses with the verb *can*.
I **can hear** the waterfall.
My dad **can't see** very well without his glasses.

8 **Circle the correct answer.**

1 I *am needing* / (need) a haircut.

2 *Do you think* / *Are you thinking* that this museum is the best?

3 Granny *is forgetting* / *forgets* my birthday every year!

4 Paul *is understanding* / *understands* the problem.

5 What *do you think* / *are you thinking* about?

6 He *doesn't remember* / *isn't remembering* her name.

7 *I hope* / *I'm hoping to* I see you soon.

8 *Is this sleeping bag belonging* / *Does this sleeping bag belong* to you?

9 They *don't seem* / *aren't seeming* to be there.

10 Yes, I *see* / *am seeing* what you mean.

9 **Complete the radio report with the present simple or present continuous.**

Hello to all our listeners!

I **1** _____am sitting_____ (sit) here in
the wildlife park, watching the elephants nearby.
They **2** _____ (have)
a nice bath in the river! There are about twenty
elephants here and there are some very young ones.
I **3** _____ (hide) behind a
tree away from the elephants so I am safe and they
4 _____ (can / not see) me.

You **5** _____ (not usually find)
elephants playing like this, but the young ones
6 _____ (love) the water.
I certainly **7** _____ (think)
the elephants **8** _____ (have)
a nice time – I would like to have a swim too!
I **9** _____ (stay)
in South Africa for a few days, so I
10 _____ (hope) to report on
more interesting wild animals like giraffes very soon!
Goodbye for now from South Africa!

10 **Read the email and correct the tenses.**

Dear Nikolas,

How are you? I'm very well. I **1** send _____am sending_____ you an email
because I **2** am wanting _____ to know your latest news.

3 Do you have _____ a good time at your new school? What subjects

4 are you liking _____ ? I **5** am going _____ to the
gym three times a week to build my muscles and I **6** learn _____ to play the
guitar this year. School is OK, but I **7** am preferring _____ the weekends!
My sister **8** studies _____ at university this year, so she is very busy.

I hope to hear from you soon.

All the best,

Alex

11 **Circle the correct answer.**

1   Milena ___ on her computer at the moment.

   a   works   b   is working   c   work

2   What time ___ you go to school in the mornings?

   a   does   b   do   c   are

3   ___ she speaking to her best friend on the phone?

   a   Is   b   Does   c   Do

4   I feel worried because I ___ about all my problems!

   a   am thinking   b   think   c   thinks

5   Peilin ___ her rubbish every day.

   a   recycle   b   is recycling   c   recycles

6   We ___ geography lessons every other day.

   a   are having   b   have   c   having

7   They ___ all their friends to the party.

   a   don't invite   b   don't inviting   c   aren't inviting

8   She ___ going shopping.

   a   doesn't like   b   isn't liking   c   likes not

Pairwork

Work in pairs. Take turns to ask and answer questions about your interests and hobbies, and what you are doing this month, this term, etc.

For example:

What do you enjoy doing in your free time?

How often do you do sport?

What subjects are you most interested in?

Are you doing any new activities this term?

Writing

Send an email to a friend, telling him/her what you are doing this year. Talk about your hobbies, your studies and what the other members of your family are doing.

Past simple: regular verbs

Affirmative	Negative	Question
I/you started	I/you did not (didn't) start	Did I/you start?
he/she/it started	he/she/it did not (didn't) start	Did he/she/it start?
we/you/they started	we/you/they did not (didn't) start	Did we/you/they start?

Short answers	
Yes, I/you did.	No, I/you didn't.
Yes, he/she/it did.	No, he/she/it didn't.
Yes, we/you/they did.	No, we/you/they didn't.

Past simple: irregular verbs

Affirmative	Negative	Question
I/you ate	I/you did not (didn't) eat	Did I/you eat?
he/she/it ate	he/she/it did not (didn't) eat	Did he/she/it eat?
we/you/they ate	we/you/they did not (didn't) eat	Did we/you/they eat?

Short answers	
Yes, I/you did.	No, I/you didn't.
Yes, he/she/it did.	No, he/she/it didn't.
Yes, we/you/they did.	No, we/you/they didn't.

We cleaned the picnic area today! We started early. We collected all the rubbish and we put it in green bags. Where were you?

I was cleaning the beach over here all morning! Look how clean it is now!

We use the past simple to talk about:

- actions that started and finished in the past.
  *She **washed** the dishes last night.*
  ***Did** you **study** the solar system last year?*

- actions that happened one after the other in the past.
  *He **opened** the fridge, **took** out the butter and **prepared** a delicious sandwich.*

- actions that were repeated or were habits in the past.
  *My mother **read** the newspaper every day.*
  *People **cooked** food on fires then.*

See the Irregular verbs list on page 198.

1 **Complete the sentences with the past simple.**

1   They _____ didn't go _____ (not go) to the cinema.

2   I _____ (post) the letters yesterday.

3   _____ (he / know) about the accident?

4   We _____ (need) a mountain rescue team to help us.

5   _____ (concert / start) on time?

6   My friend _____ (not call) last night.

7   They _____ (have) a great time at the stadium.

8   I _____ (not take) the bus to school yesterday.

2 **Match 1–8 with a–h.**

1 Where did you go last night?	a	Peter did.
2 Who won the prize?	b	No, they didn't.
3 How did you know?	c	It was really good.
4 What did you think of it?	d	It's next to the post office.
5 Didn't they say they were sorry?	e	Because Juan told me.
6 Did she decide to change her school?	f	This afternoon.
7 Where is the nearest supermarket?	g	No, I don't think so.
8 When did you arrive?	h	To the theatre.

Time expressions with the past simple

a week ago	*last year*
a month ago	*on Saturday*
a year ago	*on 29th August*, etc.
in January	*the day before yesterday*
in 1995	*the other day*
last night	*when I was five years old*
last week	*yesterday*
last summer	

Time expressions come at the beginning or the end of a sentence.

3 **Write sentences using the past simple.**

1 I / ride / a horse / in the summer holidays

   I rode a horse in the summer holidays.

2 we / have / a great party / last Saturday

   _____

3 David and Leo / win / a competition / in February

   _____

4 I / not learn / to snowboard / when / I / be / seven years old

   _____

5 Angela / leave / yesterday

   _____

6 she / send / the letter / two days / ago

   _____

7 you / watch / TV / last night / ?

   _____

8 Mateo / borrow / my chessboard / two weeks ago

   _____

Past continuous

Affirmative	Negative	Question
I was working	I was not (wasn't) working	Was I working?
you were working	you were not (weren't) working	Were you working?
he/she/it was working	he/she/it was not (wasn't) working	Was he/she/it working?
we/you/they were working	we/you/they were not (weren't) working	Were we/you/they working?

Short answers

Yes, I was.	No, I wasn't.
Yes, you were.	No, you weren't.
Yes, he/she/it was.	No, he/she/it wasn't.
Yes, we/you/they were.	No, we/you/they weren't.

We use the past continuous to talk about:

- actions that were in progress at a specific time in the past.
  *I **was watching** TV at nine o'clock yesterday.*
  *She **wasn't reading** a magazine when I saw her.*

- two or more actions that were in progress at the same time in the past.
  *Mum **was preparing** lunch and I **was doing** my homework.*
  *My brother **was playing** a game and I **was watching** him.*

- the background events in a story.
  *It **was snowing** and the wind **was blowing**.*
  *The sun **was shining** and the birds **were singing**.*

- an action in progress in the past that was interrupted by another.
  *I **was playing** football when I **fell over**.*
  *She **was having** a shower when her friend **arrived**.*

> ## Time expressions with the past continuous
>
> | | |
> |---|---|
> | *all day yesterday* | *last Sunday* |
> | *all evening* | *last year* |
> | *at ten o'clock last night* | *this morning* |

4 Complete the sentences with the past continuous.

1 She ____was talking____ (talk) on the phone for most of the evening.

2 He wasn't at home yesterday because he _____ (take) an exam.

3 We _____ (make) the salad and Adam was laying the table.

4 The baby _____ (not cry) when I went to see her.

5 No one _____ (listen) to the radio, so we turned it off.

6 The students _____ (not try) very hard because they were tired.

7 At eight o'clock on Saturday evening, they _____ (get) ready to go out.

8 It _____ (rain) all day yesterday.

9 He _____ (not read) his book – he was playing video games.

10 Dad _____ (show) Lukas how to use the internet this morning.

5 Complete the questions with the past continuous.

1 What ___were you looking for___ (you / look for) in the first-aid kit?

2 _____ (Dad / read) the newspaper all evening?

3 What _____ (he / watch) on TV last night?

4 Who _____ (phone) you at ten o'clock last night?

5 _____ (it / rain) all night last night?

6 _____ (they / study) geography last year?

7 Who _____ (he / talk) to on the phone last night?

8 _____ (you / watch) TV all day yesterday?

> ## *When* and *while*
>
> We use *when* with the past simple.
> *I was listening to the teacher **when** the fire alarm started to ring.*
> ***When** I got home, my brother was listening to music.*
>
> We use *while* with the past continuous.
> *I arrived **while** she was finishing her project.*
> ***While** I was making my bed, my best friend phoned.*

6 **Complete the sentences with *when* or *while*.**

1 I was listening to music _____while_____ I was studying.

2 _____ he called, I was getting ready to go out.

3 _____ we were eating, we talked about her studies.

4 _____ he pulled the door open, there was no one there.

5 He was reading _____ he fell asleep.

6 He was talking on his phone _____ he was fixing his bike.

7 Did you see anything interesting _____ you were at the museum?

8 It was already late _____ they got home.

> **Think about it!** 💡
>
> For an action in the past which only took a short time, we use *when*.

7 **Imagine you are Detective Whodunnit and you are investigating the crime against Mr X. In front of you is one of the main suspects, Mr Strange. Complete the questions with the past simple or the past continuous to find out exactly where he was at the time of the murder. There may be more than one possible answer.**

1 Where _____were you_____ (you / be) on the night of 12th September?

2 What _____ (you / do) between 9 and 11 p.m.?

3 Who _____ (you / be) with?

4 What _____ (you / eat) at the restaurant?

5 What _____ (you / drink)?

6 _____ (you / leave) the restaurant at any time during the evening?

7 _____ (you / know) Mr X very well?

8 _____ (you / have) any arguments with him?

8 **Use Detective Whodunnit's notes and write Mr Strange's answers to the questions in Exercise 7. There may be more than one possible answer.**

Suspect:	Mr Strange
12th September?	Blue Sky Restaurant
Between 9 and 11 p.m.?	meal at Blue Sky Restaurant
Who with?	with three friends
Food?	steak, chips, salad
Drink?	water
Left restaurant?	9–10 p.m. to pick up another friend
Know Mr X well?	good friends with him
Arguments?	no arguments

1 I was at the Blue Sky Restaurant on the night of 12th September.

2 _____

3 _____

4 _____

5 _____

6 _____

7 _____

8 _____

Used to

Affirmative	Negative	Question
I/you used to play he/she/it used to play we/you/they used to play	I/you did not (didn't) use to play he/she/it did not (didn't) use to play we/you/they did not (didn't) use to play	Did I/you use to play? Did he/she/it use to play? Did we/you/they use to play?

Short answers

Yes, I/you did.	No, I/you didn't.
Yes, he/she/it did.	No, he/she/it didn't.
Yes, we/you/they did.	No, we/you/they didn't.

We use *used to* for actions that we did regularly in the past but that we don't do now.
We also use it for states that existed in the past but that don't exist now.
*I **used to take part** in races every weekend, but now I don't have time.*
*We **used to live** in the country, but now we live in the city.*

Notes

We can use the past simple and *used to* for past habits and states that don't happen now.
There is no change in meaning, but we must use a time expression with the past simple.
*She **used to work** in the city.*
*She **worked** in the city two years ago.*

9 **Complete the sentences with the correct form of *used to* and the words in brackets.**

1 He _____ didn't use to like _____ (not like) studying, but he does now.
2 I _____ (help) my parents in the house when I had more time.
3 _____ (you / live) near the school?
4 _____ (they / have) a parrot?
5 _____ (not go) to bed late when I was younger.
6 _____ (you / watch) a lot of television?
7 She _____ (perform) acrobatics on stage.
8 They _____ (go) for walks on the hill on Sundays.
9 _____ (you / have) a lot of homework after school?
10 I _____ (play) the piano well when I was a child.

10 Rewrite the sentences using the word in bold. Use between two and five words.

1 They had a little house by the sea when they lived in Spain. **used**

They _____used to have_____ a little house by the sea.

2 During lunch, someone knocked at the door. **having**

While we _____ lunch, someone knocked at the door.

3 They watched a lot of cartoons when they were young. **used**

They _____ a lot of cartoons.

4 I could hear my brother's music playing while I was studying. **playing**

My brother _____ music while I was studying.

5 We didn't like vegetables when we were young. **use**

We _____ vegetables.

11 Six lines in the text have an extra word. Find the extra word and write it in the space.

1 One day, I was <u>always</u> walking along the road on my   _____always_____

2 way to school. It was a lovely morning; the sun it was   _____

3 shining and the birds were singing. I felt very   _____

4 happy and everything was going to well. I started to   _____

5 think about the things did I used to do when I was young.   _____

6 I used to go to school on with my bike and it was   _____

7 always a good way to start the day! My friends used to   _____

8 ride their bikes too, so we all went together. Once we   _____

9 were found a little cat on the road and we gave it   _____

10 some food because it looked really thin and hungry.   _____

12 Read the story and correct the tenses.

All of us dream of finding some lost treasure. Well, one day last summer, I **¹ was reading** _____read_____ an

article online about some treasure that was somewhere near our town! I **² wasn't telling** _____

anyone about it. I **³ was running** _____ out of the house with my phone in my hand and

⁴ was cycling _____ along a road that goes into the country. I **⁵ was going** _____

there a lot when I was a child and I **⁶ was knowing** _____ the area very well. The article said that

the person who **⁷ was wanting** _____ to find the treasure should dig under a very big old tree.

I **⁸ was finding** _____ the tree in the middle of a field. I had to find the treasure!

Pairwork

In the story in Exercise 12, there aren't any descriptive sentences about the weather, the scenery, etc. Work in pairs to write four descriptive sentences for the story and decide where they should go.

1 _____

2 _____

3 _____

4 _____

Writing

Write a story about something strange that happened to you. Remember to include both the events that happened and a description of your feelings, the scenery, etc. Use the past simple and past continuous tenses.

Present perfect simple

Affirmative

I/you have (I've/you've) started
he/she/it has (he's/she's/it's) started
we/you/they have (we've/you've/they've) started

Negative

I/you have not (haven't) started
he/she/it has not (hasn't) started
we/you/they have not (haven't) started

Question

Have I/you started?
Has he/she/it started?
Have we/you/they started?

Short answers

Yes, I/you have.   No, I/you haven't.
Yes, he/she/it has.   No, he/she/it hasn't.
Yes, we/you/they have.   No, we/you/they haven't.

The present perfect simple is formed with the verb *have/has* + past participle of the main verb.
We use the present perfect simple to talk about:

- something that happened in the past but we don't know when.
  She **has won** a prize.
  Have they **got** their exam results yet?

- something that happened in the past but is important now.
  She **has performed** in front of an audience many times.
  I **have seen** that film, so I don't want to see it again.

- something that started in the past but continues now.
  We **have lived** in this house for six years.
  He **hasn't been** at this school for long.

- something that has just happened.
  It **has** just **started** to rain.
  We **have** just **come back** from holiday.

- experiences and achievements.
  I **have visited** five different countries.
  She **has passed** her science test.

See page 198 for the Irregular verbs list.

You look really happy! What have you been doing?

I've been practising football every day. Now I'm on the school team!

That's great! Have you ever been on the team before?

No, I haven't.

1 Complete the sentences with the present perfect simple.

1 It _____ hasn't rained _____ (not rain) a lot this year.

2 She _____ (visit) England three times.

3 They _____ (not read) all the books yet.

4 We _____ (finish) lunch.

5 She _____ (do) three new experiments this week.

6 _____ (he / go) to the same school for fifteen years?

7 We _____ (take) three tests this month.

8 He _____ (not open) his presents yet.

9 _____ (I / forget) to turn off the lights again?

10 It _____ (be) really hot this month.

> ## Time expressions with the present perfect simple
>
> | | |
> |---|---|
> | *already* | *twice* |
> | *ever* | *three times* |
> | *for* | *since 1995* |
> | *for a long time/for ages* | *since June* |
> | *just* | *so far* |
> | *never* | *until now* |
> | *once* | *yet* |

2 Complete the sentences with the correct time expression from the box.

> already   ever   for   just   never
> since   so far   twice   yet

1 You don't need to make lunch. I have _____ already _____ made it.

2 Have you _____ seen an elephant?

3 We have done two units of this book _____ this year.

4 I waited _____ three hours and then I went home.

5 Emilia has _____ travelled abroad, but she wants to one day.

6 He has _____ had a shower and his hair is still wet.

7 I have read this book _____ . It was brilliant!

8 Haven't you finished doing your homework _____ ?

3 **Complete the questions with the present perfect simple. Then write answers.**

1   (you / water) ✔

_____Have you watered_____ the flowers today?

_____Yes, I have._____

2   (you ever / eat) ✗

_____ Indian food?

_____

3   (he / finish) ✔

_____ his homework?

_____

4   (you / have) ✗

_____ your dinner yet?

_____

5   (they / go) ✔

_____ to bed?

_____

6   (you / leave) ✗

_____ the cooker on?

_____

7   (you / hear) ✔

_____ the good news?

_____

8   (she ever / fly) ✔

_____ in a plane?

_____

9   (you / see) ✗

_____ the new series on TV?

_____

10   (we / make) ✗

_____ enough food for the party?

_____

Think about it!

We often use *ever* in questions with the present perfect simple and *never* in negative sentences.

Have been and *have gone*

We use *have been* to say that someone has gone to a place and has come back or that they have had an experience.
He **has been** to that restaurant twice.
She **has been** skiing before.

We use *have gone* to say that someone has gone to a place and not returned yet.
Mum **has gone** to the bank.
They **have gone** to the supermarket.

---

4 **Complete the sentences with *have/has been* or *have/has gone.***

1   She _____has gone_____ to the gym. She'll be back later.

2   I _____ to Spain on holiday a few times.

3   _____ you ever _____ to that cinema?

4   Tamaz _____ to the park. He's coming home at six o'clock.

5   Don't go to the supermarket. I _____ already _____ .

6   Where is everybody? They _____ all _____ .

7   They _____ never _____ to London, but they would like to go.

8   I thought they would be here, but they _____ already _____ .

Present perfect continuous

Affirmative

I/you have (I've/you've) been playing
he/she/it has (he's/she's/it's) been playing
we/you/they have (we've/you've/they've) been playing

Negative

I/you have not (haven't) been playing
he/she/it has not (hasn't) been playing
we/you/they have not (haven't) been playing

Question

Have I/you been playing?
Has he/she/it been playing?
Have we/you/they been playing?

Short answers

Yes, I/you have.   No, I/you haven't.
Yes, he/she/it has.   No, he/she/it hasn't.
Yes, we/you/they have.   No, we/you/they haven't.

The present perfect continuous is formed with the verb *have/has* + *been* + the main verb + *-ing*.

We use the present perfect continuous to talk about:

- something that started in the past and has happened repeatedly or has continued until now.
  *I **have been phoning** you all morning.*
  *He **has been playing** the same video game for ages!*

- something that continued over a period of time in the past and that may have finished but has results that we can see now.
  *Jana **has been running**. (She looks tired.)*
  *Mark **has been swimming**. (His hair is wet.)*

5 **Complete the sentences with the present perfect continuous.**

1 I ____have been studying____ (study) hard.
2 She _____ (cook) all morning.
3 They _____ (not live) here for very long.
4 I'm so tired! I _____ (tidy) my bedroom all day!
5 We _____ (learn) French this year.
6 Paul _____ (do) his homework for three hours.
7 They _____ (walk) around town all morning.
8 _____ (you / plan) your summer holiday?
9 The children _____ (play) quietly in their bedroom all evening.
10 I'm sorry. I _____ (not listen) to what you were saying.

Time expressions with the present perfect continuous

all day	*for years*
all night	*lately*
for a long time	*recently*
for (very) long	*since*

Notes

We use *for (very) long* in questions and negative sentences.
*Have you been waiting **for very long**?*

6   Write sentences with the present perfect continuous.

1   you / study / too much / lately
     You have been studying too much lately.

2   he / doing / his project / two weeks / for
     _____
     _____

3   we / wait / here / for a long time
     _____
     _____

4   they / prepare / for the party / all day
     _____
     _____

5   I / not read / much / recently
     _____
     _____

6   Jacob / clean / the house / since / 10 a.m.
     _____
     _____

7   Complete the questions with the present perfect continuous. Then write answers.

1   (you / cook) ✔
     _____ Have you been cooking _____ fish?
     Yes, I have.

2   (the boys / study) ✔
     _____
     hard this term?
     _____

3   (the post / arrive) ✘
     _____
     late this week?
     _____

4   (you / have) ✔
     _____
     a lot of headaches recently?
     _____

5   (the cat / eat) ✘
     _____
     more food than usual?
     _____

6   (they / play) ✘
     _____
     football this afternoon?
     _____

7   (you / buy) ✔
     _____
     a lot of things?
     _____

8   (he / try) ✔
     _____
     to fix his bike?
     _____

9   (the children / eat) ✘
     _____
     too many sweets?
     _____

10 (she / listen) ✔
     _____
     a lot of music recently?
     _____

> ## Present perfect simple or present perfect continuous?
>
> We use the present perfect simple to talk about something we have done or achieved or an action that is complete.
> I **have finished** all my homework.
> We **have written** two essays today.
>
> We use the present perfect continuous to talk about something that has lasted for a long time. It doesn't matter whether the action is complete or not.
> They **have been tidying** their bedroom all morning.
> She **has been studying** all night.

8 **Complete the sentences with the present perfect simple or the present perfect continuous.**

1 I _____ have eaten _____ (eat) three yoghurts today.
2 They _____ (play) video games all afternoon.
3 She _____ (finish) all her chores for today.
4 I _____ (be) to lots of museums.
5 We _____ (talk) about this problem for days.
6 They _____ (play) tennis all morning and they are very tired.
7 Marta _____ (study) since 6 a.m. and it's now 11 p.m.!
8 Mum _____ (buy) all the ingredients. Let's cook!
9 _____ (it / snow) all morning?
10 _____ (he / finish) his book already?

9 **Look at the table to see what the Roberts family have been doing. Then write sentences using the present perfect simple and the present perfect continuous.**

	What have they been doing?	What have they done?
Mum and Dad	do the washing up	break three plates
The boys	play football	break a window
Maria	phone her friends	not do any homework
Granny	do the housework	not clean the whole house
Grandad	read the newspaper	read half of it

1 Mum and Dad _____ have been doing the washing up. They have broken three plates _____ .
2 The boys _____ .
3 Maria _____ .
4 Granny _____ .
5 Grandad _____ .

10 **Complete the dialogue with the present perfect simple or the present perfect continuous.**

Daniel: Hi, Ivan. Where [1] _____ have you been _____ (be) all day? We
[2] _____ (look) for you!

Ivan: Hello, Daniel. Sorry, I [3] _____ (be) out all day. My basketball team
[4] _____ (train) for the big match on Saturday and I had to practise.
What [5] _____ (you / do)?

Daniel: Well, Tanya and I [6] _____ (walk) around the shops and we
[7] _____ (be) bored most of the day while we were waiting for you!
We [8] _____ (not have) anything to eat yet. Shall we go for a pizza?

Tanya: Come on, Ivan. You've been running around all day, so you must be starving! Let's go!

11 **Circle the correct answer.**

1   I *have been studying* / *have studied* hard all day long.

2   We *have invited* / *have been inviting* them to the party.

3   *Have you been eating* / *Have you eaten* all your food?

4   I *have been reading* / *have read* two books this week.

5   They *haven't been taking* / *haven't taken* any tests this week.

6   He *has been studying* / *has studied* at the library today.

7   I *have been making* / *have made* a cake. Does anybody want some?

8   *Have you sent* / *have you been sending* the email?

12 **Circle the correct answer.**

1   It ___ all night!
   a   been snowed   b   has been snowing   c   snowing

2   He ___ finished his homework yet.
   a   hasn't   b   hasn't been   c   has

3   We ___ for the bus for half an hour and it still hasn't come!
   a   have waited   b   are waiting   c   have been waiting

4   Sorry, but Martin has just ___ . Can you phone again tomorrow?
   a   left   b   leaving   c   been leaving

5   I ___ seen Alina for weeks. Do you think she's ill?
   a   hasn't   b   haven't   c   have

6   Have you ___ the news? She passed her exam!
   a   been hearing   b   heard   c   hearing

7   They haven't been to the stadium ___ a long time.
   a   for   b   since   c   about

8   I've ___ had lunch, so I'm not hungry.
   a   had already   b   already had   c   already been having

13 Complete the sentences in your own words. Use the present perfect simple or continuous.

1 I have been _____ working hard all day _____ .

2 I haven't _____ .

3 Have you _____ .

4 My mother has _____ .

5 They haven't been _____ .

6 What have you _____ ?

Pairwork

Work in pairs. Take turns to ask and answer the questions below.

- Where have you been in your country?
- Where haven't you been that you would like to go?
- Have you ever been abroad?
- Where did you go?

Writing

1 Write a short paragraph about the places you have been in your country and abroad. Write about the places you haven't been to.

2 Write a short paragraph about what you have been doing or what you have done today.

Past perfect simple and past perfect continuous

Past perfect simple

Affirmative	Negative	Question
I/you had (I'd/you'd) stopped he/she/it had (he'd/she'd/it'd) stopped we/you/they had (we'd/you'd/ they'd) stopped	I/you had not (hadn't) stopped he/she/it had not (hadn't) stopped we/you/they had not (hadn't) stopped	Had I/you stopped? Had he/she/it stopped? Had we/you/they stopped?

Short answers	
Yes, I/you had.	No, I/you hadn't.
Yes, he/she/it had.	No, he/she/it hadn't.
Yes, we/you/they had.	No, we/you/they hadn't.

The past perfect simple is formed with the verb *had* + past participle of the main verb.
We use the past perfect simple to talk about:

- an action that happened before another action in the past.
  Sam **had studied** hard for a month before he took his exams.
  Had Paula **finished** her homework before the film started?

- an action that happened before a specific time in the past.
  They **had done** the shopping before lunchtime.
  Linda **had made** the food for the party by four o'clock.

See page 198 for the Irregular verbs list.

I saw you outside the Head Teacher's office yesterday. You looked really tired!

Yes! I'd just finished my Maths exam. It was difficult!

1 **Complete the sentences with the past perfect simple.**

1 I _____had eaten_____ (eat) three biscuits before lunch.

2 They _____ (stay) up very late the night before, so they couldn't get up in the morning.

3 I _____ (look) at lots of pictures before I found one I really liked.

4 The team were sad because they _____ (not lose) any other matches in the tournament.

5 _____ (they / already leave) the restaurant when you got there?

6 They _____ (have) their lunch by the time Damian came home from school.

7 She _____ (not do) all her homework by nine o'clock, so she left some for later.

8 He _____ (not open) his presents yet, so he was very excited.

Time expressions with the past perfect simple

after
already
as soon as
before
by (a time or date)
by the time
just … when
never … (before)
when

*After we **had been** to the supermarket, we went home.*
*As soon as he **had arrived** at the airport, he checked in for his flight.*
*By the time Angela **had woken up**, it was lunchtime.*
*She **had** never **seen** a tiger before she went to Africa.*

Notes

We use the word *by* to talk about an activity that had been completed before a specific time in the past.
*He **had eaten** his lunch **by** two o'clock.*

Past perfect simple or past simple?

When we talk about two or more actions in the past, we use the past perfect simple to emphasise that one action had finished before the other(s). For the other action(s), we use the past simple.
*She **had done** all the ironing before she went out.*
*Before he went to school, he **had taken** the dog for a walk.*

2 **Rewrite the two sentences as one sentence. Use the words in brackets.**

1 The rain stopped. They went out for a walk. (after)

 After the rain had stopped, they went out for a walk.

2 They finished their homework. It was nine o'clock. (by)

 _____

3 Klaudia saved up her money. She went shopping. (before)

 _____

4 She finished talking on the phone. They watched the film. (after)

 _____

5 The police got to the bank. The robbers had got away. (by the time)

 _____

6 She finished eating her dinner. She invited her friend around. (as soon as)

 _____

7 They built their house in the countryside. They moved out of the city. (when)

 _____

8 Misha turned his computer on. There was a power cut. (just ... when)

 _____

Past perfect continuous

Affirmative	Negative	Question
I had (I'd) been playing	I had not (hadn't) been playing	Had I been playing?
you had (you'd) been playing	you had not (hadn't) been playing	Had you been playing?
he had (he'd) been playing	he had not (hadn't) been playing	Had he been playing?
she had (she'd) been playing	she had not (hadn't) been playing	Had she been playing?
it had (it'd) been playing	it had not (hadn't) been playing	Had it been playing?
we had (we'd) been playing	we had not (hadn't) been playing	Had we been playing?
you had (you'd) been playing	you had not (hadn't) been playing	Had you been playing?
they had (they'd) been playing	they had not (hadn't) been playing	Had they been playing?

Short answers	
Yes, I/you had.	No, I/you hadn't.
Yes, he/she/it had.	No, he/she/it hadn't.
Yes, we/you/they had.	No, we/you/they hadn't.

The past perfect continuous is formed with *had* + *been* + main verb + *-ing*.
We use the past perfect continuous:

* to talk about an action that was in progress before another action in the past.
 *The garden looked beautiful because we **had been working** hard in it all weekend.*
 *Katie **had been studying** hard before her exams so she did well.*

* to show that one action in the past lasted for a long time before another past action.
 *I **had been looking** for my watch for ages when Celia found it.*
 *She **had been playing** tennis for two hours, so she had a shower.*

3 **Complete the sentences with the past perfect continuous.**

1   They _____had been travelling_____ (travel) for two hours when the car broke down.

2   Mum _____ (warm up) the food in the oven when the family arrived.

3   Everyone _____ (have) such a great time at the party that they didn't want to leave.

4   I _____ (sleep) for an hour when I woke up.

5   We _____ (not do) our homework for very long when you arrived.

6   She _____ (not feel) well for weeks when she went into hospital.

7   The children _____ (sit) quietly when one of them started crying.

8   He _____ (play) for the team for a month when they made him captain.

9   Mike _____ (not do) his homework properly, so the teacher called his parents.

10   I _____ (not use) my mobile phone for long when it stopped working.

4 **Complete the questions with the past perfect continuous.**

1   _____Had they been trying_____ (they / try) to phone us all day?

2   _____ (she / walk) to the park when it started to rain?

3   What _____ (they / plan) to do in the evening?

4   _____ (you / buy) a lot of new clothes when I saw you?

5   _____ (she / practise) a lot before the concert? She was very good!

6   _____ (you / live) in that house for a long time before you moved?

7   _____ (they / cook) for three days? There was so much food!

8   Where _____ (you / look for) him?

9   _____ (he / swim) after lunch every day?

10   _____ (it / snow) all night in the mountains?

Think about it!

The form of the past perfect simple and past perfect continuous is the same for all subjects: *I, you, he/she/it, we, you/they.*

Past perfect simple or past perfect continuous?

We use both the past perfect simple and the past perfect continuous to show that one action had finished before another in the past. The difference is that we use the past perfect continuous to emphasise the length of time an action lasted for.

5 **Complete the text with the past simple, past perfect simple or past perfect continuous.**

Last night, my friends, Judy and Paul, [1] _____told_____ (tell) me all

about the holiday they [2] _____ (have) at a wildlife sanctuary in

southern India two years ago. They [3] _____ (want) to go there

for many years, but they [4] _____ (never have) enough money

before. They [5] _____ (save) up for three years before they

finally [6] _____ (go) on the trip last year.

The holiday organisers [7] _____ (explain) to them

before they [8] _____ (arrive) there that they would

spend the night in a campsite in the middle of the jungle, but when Judy

[9] _____ (hear) that snakes might come as visitors during the

night, she was a bit worried! The organisers [10] _____ (not give)

them that information before they [11] _____ (book) the holiday!

In the end, they [12] _____ (have) a fantastic time.

When they [13] _____ (come) back home, they

[14] _____ (tell) us how they [15] _____ (see)

elephants swimming, leopards hunting and lions sleeping in the hot sun. Obviously, it

[16] _____ (be) the holiday of a lifetime!

6 **Circle the correct answer.**

1   She *had been having* / *had* a nightmare last night after watching a scary film on TV.

2   He *had arrived* / *had been arriving* at the party a long time before anyone else came.

3   They had finished their lunch by the time Mum *had come* / *came* home.

4   When they got home, they found that someone *broke* / *had broken* into their house.

5   She *had been talking* / *had talked* on the phone for ages when she realised the line was dead.

6   She was unhappy because she *had been losing* / *had lost* her favorite bracelet.

7   They *had been waiting* / *waited* for the bus for a long time before one arrived.

8   After Symon *had tidied* / *had been tidying* his room, his mum came to look at it.

7 **Complete the sentences with the words from the box.**

| after   been   before   by   ~~didn't~~   had (x2)   hadn't |

1   He hadn't _____been_____ listening to the teacher, so he _____didn't_____ know what to do.

2   They _____ cooked lunch by one o'clock.

3   We _____ finished getting ready _____ the time the bus came, so we missed it.

4   The boys _____ been playing football all afternoon and they came home covered in mud.

5   _____ Tony had been swimming for an hour, he felt very tired.

6   Marisa had put on her coat _____ she went out.

8 **Complete the text with the past simple, past perfect simple or past perfect continuous.**

Last Saturday, I ¹ _____went_____ (go) with my friends to the
fairground. By the evening, we ² _____ (be) on most of the
rides and we ³ _____ (spend) most of our money! My friends
and I ⁴ _____ (eat) hot dogs and ice creams all day and it
⁵ _____ (be) nearly time to go home when we suddenly
⁶ _____ (realise) my little brother, Ben, ⁷ _____ (be)
not with us. He ⁸ _____ (want) to come to the fairground with us and he
⁹ _____ (be) quite happy following us around all afternoon. But now, he
¹⁰ _____ (disappear)! Where ¹¹ _____ (he / go)?
We ¹² _____ (look) everywhere in the fairground, but he
¹³ _____ (not be) anywhere. I ¹⁴ _____ (start)
to feel very anxious because I ¹⁵ _____ (love) Ben and I
certainly ¹⁶ _____ (not want) anything bad to happen to him.
Just then, we ¹⁷ _____ (hear) shouts coming from the
Big Wheel. We all ¹⁸ _____ (run) over there – and what
¹⁹ _____ (we / see)? Ben was sitting on one of the seats on the Big
Wheel that was up in the air and was now coming down again! Everyone was pointing at
Ben and looking worried. I ²⁰ _____ (go) to get him off the wheel
and we quickly ²¹ _____ (disappear) into the crowd. When we
²² _____ (get) home, nobody ²³ _____ (believe)
Ben when he ²⁴ _____ (say) that he ²⁵ _____ (be)
on the Big Wheel all on his own!

Pairwork

**Work in pairs. Take turns to ask and answer questions about what you had done before each
of the times or days below.**

- eight o'clock this morning
- ten o'clock last night
- two weeks ago
- last year
- last Saturday
- your last birthday

For example:
*By eight o'clock this morning, Helen **had eaten** her breakfast.*

Writing

**Write an entry in your diary for one day last week. Say what happened on that day, what
had happened and what you had been doing before that day. Use the three tenses you have
been practising in this unit.**

1 Complete the sentences with the present simple.

1   He ___doesn't speak___ (not speak) Spanish.

2   _____ (you / come) from Russia.

3   I _____ (go) to school every day during the week.

4   They _____ (not watch) TV during meal times.

5   Snow _____ (melt) when the sun shines.

6   _____ (he / see) his friends at the weekend?

7   They _____ (not eat) eat a lot of meat.

8   _____ (it / be) cold in your country in the winter?

2 Rewrite the sentences with the adverbs of frequency in the right place.

1   Does she phone her brother? (often)

   Does she often phone her brother?

2   Is she late for her lessons? (always)

   _____

   _____

3   He plays computer games. (sometimes)

   _____

   _____

4   I ride my bike in the park. (rarely)

   _____

   _____

5   Is it dangerous to swim after eating? (always)

   _____

   _____

6   Samuel plays football in the summer. (never)

   _____

   _____

7   We see my cousins who live in Canada. (rarely)

   _____

   _____

8   Does your family eat in restaurants? (often)

   _____

   _____

3 Complete the sentences with the verbs from the box. Use the present continuous.

> concentrate   ~~eat~~   get   not live
> make   plan   stay   wash

1   He ___is eating___ at the moment. Can you call back later?

2   She had a cold, but she _____ better now.

3   I _____ . Please don't interrupt me.

4   My father _____ his car. He does it every Saturday.

5   He _____ in England anymore. He's moved to Italy.

6   _____ you _____ a surprise party for them?

7   I _____ him a cake for his birthday.

8   They _____ with us for a few days.

4 Circle the correct answer.

1 He *likes* / *is liking* all sports, especially football.
2 I *think* / *am thinking* you're right.
3 She is a waitress. She *works* / *is working* very long hours.
4 That bicycle *belongs* / *is belonging* to Andrea.
5 We *stay* / *are staying* at a hotel during the holidays.
6 I *can't hear* / *am not hearing* what you are saying.
7 It *is always raining* / *always rains* in the winter.
8 She *doesn't know* / *is not knowing* the answer.

5 Complete the sentences with the past simple.

1 I _____didn't see_____ (not see) him yesterday.
2 We _____ (not have) any problems with the science test.
3 She _____ (show) me a photo of the beautiful butterfly.
4 The baby _____ (sleep) all night long.
5 _____ (you / go) on holiday in August?
6 I _____ (see) my best friend from primary school yesterday.
7 Those boys _____ (not break) the window.
8 _____ (you / buy) those boots you saw in the shop?

6 Complete the sentences with the past continuous.

1 The students _____were listening_____ (listen) to music this morning.
2 The wind _____ (blow) hard when they left the house.
3 I _____ (not run) very fast, but I soon got tired.
4 What _____ (you / look) at with your friend?
5 We _____ (come) home from school when we heard the news.
6 Who _____ (you / talk) to on the phone?
7 They _____ (try) to phone us all day, but we were out.
8 She _____ (not have) a very good time at the party, so she left early.

7 Complete the sentences with the correct form of *used to* and the verbs from the box.

> chase   ~~have~~   not know   like   practise   tell   travel   not walk

1 She _____used to have_____ a cat, but she doesn't have any pets now.
2 _____ you _____ abroad a lot?
3 We _____ a lot, but now we prefer it to taking the bus.
4 He _____ a lot of jokes, but nobody laughed at them!
5 _____ she _____ playing with toys?
6 The cat _____ birds, but it's too old now.
7 My mum _____ anything about computers, but now she's an expert.
8 My sister _____ the piano for three hours a day when she was younger.

8 **Complete the sentences with the present perfect simple.**

1   He __hasn't written__ (not write) his essay yet.

2   They _____ (forget) to buy him a present for his birthday!

3   There _____ (be) a lot of rain this month.

4   I _____ (read) all these books for school.

5   We _____ (not see) Jarek recently.

6   They _____ (live) here for ten years.

7   They _____ (run) five miles. They're really tired!

8   _____ (you / buy) any new video games recently?

9 **Complete the sentences with the verbs from the box. Use the present perfect continuous.**

> go   have   ~~look for~~   not live   play
> study   teach   try

1   They ___have been looking for___ you all morning!

2   I _____ to do this maths problem for an hour. It's difficult!

3   How long _____ he _____ ? He has been in his room for ages!

4   She _____ to the gym since February. She looks great!

5   They _____ here very long, so they don't know many people.

6   He _____ at this school since September. The pupils love him!

7   I _____ guitar lessons for ten months.

8   He _____ football – that's why he's so dirty!

10 **Circle the correct answer.**

1   I have ___ for three hours and I still haven't finished.

   a   worked

   b   been working

   c   working

2   We ___ all our jobs yet.

   a   haven't

   b   haven't done

   c   have done

3   She ___ for the competition for months.

   a   has training

   b   is training

   c   has been training

4   No, Nick isn't here. He ___ out to the shops.

   a   has left

   b   has gone

   c   has been

5   Haven't you finished ___ ?

   a   yet

   b   already

   c   just

6   She ___ the bicycle. You can take it out for a ride if you want.

   a   has been fixing

   b   already fixed

   c   has fixed

7   I have lived in this house ___ I was born.

   a   always

   b   for

   c   since

8   Have you ___ tried water-skiing?

   a   ever

   b   still

   c   before

11 **Complete the sentences with the past perfect simple.**

1 He _____had lost_____ (lose) his keys and I couldn't find them anywhere.

2 She _____ (phone) her mum before she had gone out.

3 _____ (they / leave) the party when you got there?

4 We _____ (take) some great photos before it started to rain.

5 _____ (they / do) their homework before their dad got home?

6 _____ (he / cook) dinner by the time you arrived?

7 I _____ (not be) there before, so I didn't know anyone.

8 They _____ (eat) almost half of the cake by dinnertime!

12 **Circle the correct answer.**

1 He was happy because he *had found* / *had been finding* his watch.

2 My friends *have been moving* / *moved* here last year.

3 They *looked* / *had been looking* for her all morning but still hadn't found her by lunchtime.

4 When they *had been studying* / *studied* for two hours, their mum let them have a break.

5 Yesterday, my uncle *brought* / *had been bringing* a lot of presents for us!

6 I *had been cooking* / *had cooked* for the party for two days.

7 They *had started* / *had been starting* supper by the time their dad came home.

8 She *had been watching* / *had watched* TV all morning before her mum told her to do her homework.

13 **Complete the sentences with the verbs from the box. Use the past perfect continuous.**

| eat | go | play | snowboarding | ~~not study~~ | rain | walk | win |

1 They ___hadn't been studying___ at all, so I wasn't surprised when they failed their exams.

2 Where _____ he _____ ? His shoes were very dirty.

3 It _____ for three days before it finally stopped.

4 She _____ sweets all morning – that's why she wasn't hungry.

5 They were wet because they _____ tennis in the rain.

6 The team _____ the game until the other team scored a goal.

7 I _____ to that school for five years when I met my best friend.

8 She _____ for the first time, so she had fallen over a lot.

Future tenses (1)

Present continuous: future meaning

Affirmative	Negative	Question
I am (I'm) travelling	I am not (I'm not) travelling	Am I travelling?
you are (you're) travelling	you are not (aren't) travelling	Are you travelling?
he/she/it is (he's/she's/it's) travelling	he/she/it is not (isn't) travelling	Is he/she/it travelling?
we/you/they are (we're/you're/they're) travelling	we/you/they are not (aren't) travelling	Are we/you/they travelling?

Short answers

Yes, I am.	No, I'm not.
Yes, you are.	No, you aren't.
Yes, he/she/it is.	No, he/she/it isn't.
Yes, we/you/they are.	No, we/you/they aren't.

We can use the present continuous to talk about plans and arrangements in the near future.
*She's **seeing** her grandma next week.*
*I**'m looking after** my neighbour's children on Saturday.*

Are you getting your new computer soon?

Yes, I'm getting it next week.

1 **Write sentences with the present continuous.**

1 I / cook / lunch / tomorrow

I am cooking lunch tomorrow.

2 I / meet / my new teacher / on Monday

_____

_____

3 Natalia / buy / a new bike / at the weekend

_____

_____

4 she / stay / with her friend / next weekend

_____

_____

5 my brother / work / in the supermarket / on Saturday

_____

_____

6 he / leave / the USA / in the summer

_____

_____

7 we / go / to the beach / tomorrow

_____

_____

8 they / have / a history lesson / at three o'clock this afternoon

_____

_____

2 **Write questions with the verbs from the box. Use the present continuous.**

buy	go	have	help	make	~~paint~~
		repair	take		

1 _____Is_____ he _____painting_____ his bedroom at the weekend?

2 _____ you _____ a party on Friday?

3 _____ Mum _____ a special meal for your birthday tomorrow?

4 _____ she _____ her friend with her on the trip?

5 _____ they _____ some new clothes next weekend?

6 _____ Sandra _____ her dad to clean the car today?

7 _____ we _____ to the beach this afternoon?

8 _____ you _____ your broken bike at the weekend?

Present simple: future meaning

Affirmative	Negative	Question
I/you travel	I/you do not (don't) travel	Do I/you travel?
he/she/it travels	he/she/it does not (doesn't) travel	Does he/she/it travel?
we/you/they travel	we/you/they do not (don't) travel	Do we/you/they travel?

Short answers

Yes, I/you do.	No, I/you don't.
Yes, he/she/it does.	No, he/she/it doesn't.
Yes, we/you/they do.	No, we/you/they don't.

We can use the present simple to talk about timetables and programmed events in the future.
*The coach to the football game **leaves** at eleven o'clock tomorrow morning.*
*The film **doesn't begin** until 7:30 tonight.*

3 **Complete the sentences with the present simple.**

1 The bus _____arrives_____ (arrive) at five thirty this afternoon.

2 The plane _____ (land) at seven o'clock tomorrow morning.

3 The train _____ (not leave) for another hour.

4 The concert _____ (finish) after midnight on Saturday, so we'll be tired.

5 The film _____ (start) at nine o'clock this evening.

6 What time _____ your plane _____ (take off)?

7 My first piano lesson _____ (begin) in half an hour.

8 My friend _____ (arrive) at eight o'clock tomorrow night.

4 **Make the sentences negative.**

1 The theatre opens at six o'clock on Saturday.

The theatre doesn't open at six o'clock on Saturday.

2 The restaurant closes at midnight tonight.

_____

3 Our English lesson starts at half past five tomorrow.

_____

4 The plane takes off at nine o'clock this evening.

_____

5 The train departs in half an hour.

_____

6 School starts at ten o'clock tomorrow morning.

_____

Future simple

Affirmative	Negative	Question
I/you will (I'll/you'll) travel he/she/it will (he'll/she'll/it'll) travel we/you/they will (we'll/you'll/they'll) travel	I/you will not (won't) travel he/she/it will not (won't) travel we/you/they will not (won't) travel	Will I/you travel? Will he/she/it travel? Will we/you/they travel?

Short answers	
Yes, I/you will.	No, I/you won't.
Yes, he/she/it will.	No, he/she/it won't.
Yes, we/you/they will.	No, we/you/they won't.

We use the future simple for:

- predictions.
  I think she'll get that computer she's been wanting.

- decisions made at the time of speaking.
  It's too dark in here; I'll turn on the lights.

- promises.
  I'll wash up every day for a month.
  Will you write to me every day?

- threats.
  Do your homework or I'll take your laptop away!
  Be quiet or I'll call the police!

Notes

We only use *shall* with *I* and *we* in questions when we want to offer to do something or when we suggest something.
Shall I make supper tonight?
Shall we watch a film this evening?

---

5 **Rewrite the sentences with *will* or *shall* in the correct place.**

1 I get you something to eat?
  Shall I get you something to eat?

2 I think it be hot tomorrow.
  _____
  _____

3 Don't make a mess or you not go out tonight!
  _____
  _____

4 I help you with your homework later, I promise.
  _____
  _____

5 Look! It's snowing! I think I go for a walk.
  _____
  _____

6 You take care of my cat while I'm on holiday?
  _____
  _____

7 She not give the money back.
  _____
  _____

8 We play a different game now?
  _____
  _____

Think about it!

We use *shall* instead of *will* for offers or suggestions with *I* and *we*.

6 **Circle the correct answer.**

1 We *will go* / *are going* to the park to play football.
2 *Are you coming* / *Do you come* out with us on Saturday?
3 The show *will begin* / *begins* at eight o'clock.
4 Does the train leave at seven? Yes, it *does* / *is*.
5 We *will have* / *are having* an English lesson tomorrow.
6 *Shall* / *Will* we go for a walk?
7 That exercise looks difficult. I *will help* / *am helping* you with it.
8 We *are having* / *will have* a party next weekend.

Be going to

Affirmative

I am (I'm) going to travel
you are (you're) going to travel
he/she/it is (he's/she's/it's) going to travel
we/you/they are (we're/you're/they're) going to travel

Negative

I am not (I'm not) going to travel
you are not (aren't) going to travel
he/she/it is not (isn't) going to travel
we/you/they are not (aren't) going to travel

Question

Am I going to travel?
Are you going to travel?
Is he/she/it going to travel?
Are we/you/they going to travel?

Short answers

Yes, I am.
Yes, you are.
Yes, he/she/it is.
Yes, we/you/they are.

No, I'm not.
No, you aren't
No, he/she/it isn't.
No, we/you/they aren't.

We use *be going to* to talk about:

- plans and arrangements in the near future.
  *We **are going to stay** on a farm for our holiday this summer.*

- something we know is going to happen because we have evidence.
  *Be careful! That glass jar **is going to fall**.*

Notes

We can use both *be going* to and the present continuous to talk about plans and arrangements.
***I'm going to visit** my friend tomorrow.*
***I'm visiting** my friend tomorrow.*

---

7 **Complete the sentences with the correct form of *be going to* and the verbs from the box.**

build   buy   fail   go   have   snow   start   study

1 He _____ is going to buy _____ a new laptop next year.
2 They _____ all weekend for their exams.
3 Dad _____ training at the gym because he wants to get fit.
4 Kenji _____ a tree house for his little sister.
5 I _____ a shower and go to bed.
6 Where _____ you _____ after school today?
7 You _____ all your exams if you don't study harder.
8 Look at the sky! I think it _____ tonight!

8 Write questions. Then write answers using the verb in brackets.

1   you / buy / the birthday cake / later today (make)

   Are you going to buy the birthday cake later
   today?
   No, I'm going to make it.

2   she / learn / Italian / next year (teach)

   _____

   _____

   _____

3   we / earn / some money / in the summer (spend)

   _____

   _____

   _____

4   the doctor / examine / the patient / this evening (visit)

   _____

   _____

   _____

5   you / read / the email / today (send)

   _____

   _____

   _____

6   he / play / football / next summer (watch)

   _____

   _____

   _____

7   I / buy / the presents / for my birthday (receive)

   _____

   _____

   _____

8   Gabriel / wash / the walls (paint)

   _____

   _____

   _____

9 Complete the sentences with the correct form of *be going to* or the future simple and the verb in brackets.

1   Brian _____is studying_____ (study) art at college. Do you think he _____will be_____ (be) a famous artist one day?

2   I _____ (go) shopping this weekend. I promise I _____ (bring) you something nice!

3   It _____ (be) a lovely day. _____ you _____ (help) me wash the car?

4   Mum _____ (order) the food now. I _____ (have) noodles!

5   **A:** Olga is eating a lot of chocolate. She _____ (feel) sick soon.

   B: OK, I _____ (get) her a glass of water.

6   **A:** _____ you _____ (come) to the barbecue next weekend?

   B: I don't know. I _____ (decide) on Friday night.

7   **A:** We're late! We _____ (miss) the bus!

   B: Never mind. We _____ (take) a taxi.

8   **A:** _____ you _____ (phone) me tonight?

   B: No, I can't. I _____ (visit) my cousins.

10 **Circle the correct answer.**

1 What ___ at the weekend?

   a you do   (b) are you doing   c will you do

2 I don't think this party ___ much fun.

   a will be   b is being   c is going to

3 ___ buy a new pair of jeans today?

   a Are you   b Will you be   c Are you going to

4 He ___ to the doctor this evening about his cough.

   a is going to   b is going   c will go

5 Our teacher ___ us to the science museum next Saturday.

   a is taking   b will to take   c takes

6 That bag looks heavy. ___ I carry it for you?

   a Do   b Shall   c Am

7 She looks very sad. I think she ___ cry.

   a will   b shall   c is going to

8 The baseball coach ___ explain the rules of the game before you play.

   a is   b will   c does

11 **Complete the dialogue with one word in each gap.**

Sandor: What ¹_____are_____ you doing at the weekend, Bela?

Bela: Nothing much. What about you?

Sandor: I'm ²_____ to go to the rock concert. My brother bought me two tickets for my birthday.

Bela: Lucky you! I'm sure you ³_____ both enjoy the concert a lot.

Sandor: Yes, I think it ⁴_____ be a brilliant concert. But my brother ⁵_____ not coming with me.

Bela: Why not?

Sandor: He's ⁶_____ out with his friends tomorrow.

Bela: So, you're ⁷_____ to go on your own?

Sandor: No, I ⁸_____ taking a friend.

Bela: That ⁹_____ be nice. Who ¹⁰_____ you giving the ticket to?

Sandor: You! ¹¹_____ you come to the concert with me?

Bela: Me? Yes, I'd love to come! What time ¹²_____ the concert start?

Sandor: It ¹³_____ at nine o'clock, so I ¹⁴_____ pick you up at half past eight.

Bela: Fantastic! I ¹⁵_____ see you tomorrow!

12 **Find the mistakes in the sentences. Then write them correctly.**

1   Are you <u>go</u> anywhere fun tonight?

Are you going anywhere fun tonight?

2   I'm thirsty. I think I'm going to have some water.

3   Shall you help me carry the shopping, please?

4   I'm sure you won't to fail your exams.

5   Which planets are astronauts going exploring in the future?

6   **A:** Are you going swimming on Saturday?

     B: No, I won't.

Pairwork

Work in pairs. Take turns to ask and answer questions about the future.

For example:

What will your town or city be like in the year 2200?

What do you think is going to happen to our planet in two hundred years?

What are your friends and family doing tomorrow?

Writing

Write a magazine article about what you think life will be like on Earth in the year 2200. Use your answers from the Pairwork exercise above to help you.

Future tenses (2)

Future continuous

Affirmative	Negative	Question
I will (I'll) be swimming	I will not (won't) be swimming	Will I be swimming?
you will (you'll) be swimming	you will not (won't) be swimming	Will you be swimming?
he will (he'll) be swimming	he will not (won't) be swimming	Will he be swimming?
she will (she'll) be swimming	she will not (won't) be swimming	Will she be swimming?
it will (it'll) be swimming	it will not (won't) be swimming	Will it be swimming?
we will (we'll) be swimming	we will not (won't) be swimming	Will we be swimming?
you will (you'll) be swimming	you will not (won't) be swimming	Will you be swimming?
they will (they'll) be swimming	they will not (won't) be swimming	Will they be swimming?

Short answers

Yes, I/you will.	No, I won't
Yes, he/she/it will.	No, you won't.
Yes, we/you/they will.	No, he/she/it won't.
	No, we/you/they won't.

We use the future continuous to talk about something that will be in progress at a specific time in the future.

*This time next week, we **will be going** back to school.*
***Will** they **be dancing** at ten o'clock on Saturday night?*

What will you be doing this time next week?

I'll be relaxing at the beach and reading lots of books!

1 **Complete the sentences with the future continuous.**

1 Tomorrow morning, I _____ will be taking _____ (take) my English exam.

2 This time next week, they _____ (travel) to the mountains.

3 At four o'clock this afternoon, she _____ (have) her guitar lesson.

4 Tomorrow afternoon, you _____ (eat) pizza at my house!

5 Next Monday morning, my dad _____ (fly) to Thailand.

6 In two hours we _____ (watch) the concert.

7 He _____ (play) basketball all Saturday afternoon.

8 I _____ (sit) on the beach next week.

2 **Make the sentences negative.**

1 You will be watching that film all afternoon.

   You won't be watching that film all afternoon.

2 They will be doing their homework this evening.

   _____

3 I'll be waiting outside the cinema at two o'clock.

   _____

4 We'll be taking our French test on Thursday.

   _____

5 People will be flying cars in the next year.

   _____

6 People will be living on other planets in ten years' time.

   _____

3 **Write questions.**

1 they / sleep / at midnight / ?

   Will they be sleeping at midnight?

2 you / go / to a new school / next year / ?

   _____

3 you / do / homework / for three hours / ?

   _____

4 you / go / to the beach / when you're on holiday / ?

   _____

5 Dad / make / dinner / when / we get home / ?

   _____

6 the boys / ride / their bikes / this afternoon / ?

   _____

4 **Write questions. Then write answers using the verb in brackets. Use the future continuous.**

1 they / dance / at the party (sing)

   Will they be dancing at the party?

   No, they won't. They'll be singing.

2 you / read / for the next hour (write)

   _____

   _____

3 we / sail / to France / this time tomorrow (fly)

   _____

   _____

4 the teacher / give out / the tests / this afternoon (mark)

   _____

   _____

5 she / dig / the garden / at seven o'clock / this evening (water)

   _____

   _____

6 the students / relax / all day (study)

   _____

   _____

7 you / walk / to work / tomorrow (drive)

   _____

   _____

8 he / act / in the play / on Saturday (dance)

   _____

   _____

5 **Complete the sentences with the verbs from the box. Use the future continuous.**

> not buy   not cycle   ~~not have~~   play   not sing   study   wear   work

1 It's raining. We _____won't be having_____ a picnic this afternoon.

2 She has a sore throat. She _____ in the concert tomorrow night.

3 He's lost his wallet. He _____ any new video games this weekend.

4 Dad's very busy. He _____ until nine o'clock this evening.

5 I've got an exam tomorrow. I _____ all day today!

6 I'll meet you at the park. I _____ a red T-shirt so you will easily see me.

7 His bike has a flat tyre. He _____ to school this week.

8 Today is the last day of school. This time tomorrow, I _____ with my friends!

6 Write sentences.

1 At 9 a.m. tomorrow, Shari will be making breakfast.
2 _____
3 _____
4 _____
5 _____
6 _____
7 _____
8 _____

Shari's diary – tomorrow

9 a.m.   make breakfast

11 a.m.   clean my room

1 p.m.   write emails

2 p.m.   eat lunch

4 p.m.   practise the piano

5 p.m.   go to my piano lesson

7 p.m.   have dinner

11 p.m.   go to bed

Future simple or future continuous?

We use the future simple to talk about something (a prediction, an offer, a sudden decision, a promise) that will happen and be completed in the future.
I think you'll live to a very old age.
I'll help you with those boxes.

We use the future continuous to talk about something that will be in progress at a specific time in the future.
This time tomorrow, we'll be writing our maths test.
What will you be doing at eight o'clock tonight?

7 Complete the sentences with the future simple or the future continuous.

1 I'm sure it _____ will be _____ (be) sunny tomorrow.
2 On Monday evening, she _____ (play) in the concert.
3 I know they _____ (not make) their beds before they go out.
4 _____ you _____ (finish) the washing up for me?
5 I don't feel well. I think I _____ (lie) down for half an hour.
6 What _____ you _____ (do) on Saturday night?
7 _____ you always _____ (be) my friend?
8 How many people _____ (swim) in the competition next week?
9 This time next week, they _____ (relax) on the beach.
10 If he's lucky, he _____ (pass) his maths test.

Think about it!

Will the action be in progress in the future? Use the future continuous.

8 **Complete the sentences with the words from the box.**

> be   compete   competing   take
> taking   watch   watching   won't

1   They'll _____be_____ having breakfast at eight o'clock tomorrow morning.

2   I'm sure it _____ rain tomorrow, so let's arrange to go to the beach.

3   Everybody will be _____ the football match on Saturday.

4   Where will the Olympics _____ place in the future?

5   Which teams will be _____ in the final competition?

6   At nine o'clock tomorrow, I'll be _____ my English exam.

7   He'll _____ in the Olympics when he's older.

8   You go and play tennis, and I'll _____ you.

9 **Circle the correct answer.**

1   Do you think people ___ electric cars in the future?
    a   will driving   b   to drive   c   will drive

2   On Saturday evening, we will ___ to America.
    a   fly   b   be flying   c   flying

3   My dad says that it ___ foggy this evening.
    a   will   b   will being   c   will be

4   What do you think you ___ at five o'clock tomorrow afternoon?
    a   do   b   will be doing   c   will do

5   I promise I will ___ home before you go to bed.
    a   will be being   b   will be   c   be

6   ___ you ever learn Japanese?
    a   Will   b   Will you   c   You will

7   That looks difficult! ___ you?
    a   Shall I help   b   Shall I be helping   c   Shall help

8   ___ next week, she will be at the beach.
    a   This time   b   Soon   c   At

10 **Complete the text with the words from the box.**

> be   cook   staying   studying   this (x2)   will   won't

On Saturday, my parents are going on holiday to France – [1] _____this_____ time next week, they will be [2] _____ in an expensive hotel and they will [3] _____ learning to speak French. I [4] _____ be with them because I'll be [5] _____ hard for my exams. My grandmother [6] _____ be staying with me. She will [7] _____ all the meals and clean the house while my parents are away.

[8] _____ time next year, I will be going with them and it will be great!

11 **Find the mistakes in the sentences. Then write them correctly.**

1　What will <u>you doing</u> ten years from now?

　　<u>What will you be doing ten years from now?</u>

2　What time will you be being home this afternoon?

　　_____

3　At nine o'clock this evening, will you studying?

　　_____

4　I'll be doing that for you!

　　_____

5　Do you think it will rain when we get up in the morning?

　　_____

6　How often you visit your grandparents?

　　_____

7　Will you to be working on Monday?

　　_____

8　I'm very hungry. I think I'll be having a sandwich.

　　_____

Pairwork

Work in pairs. Take turns to ask and answer questions about the future. Think about the points below.

- what you will be doing this time next year
- where you will be this time next month
- what you will be doing at seven o'clock on Saturday night
- what you think the weather will be like next week

Writing

Write a short paragraph about what you think your life will be like ten years from now. Use the future continuous. Think about the points below.

- which city you will be living in
- what kind of house you will be living in
- what you will be studying
- what your family and friends will be doing

Countable and uncountable nouns

Countable nouns

Most nouns are countable and have a singular and plural form.

table	→	tables		dress	→	dresses
lady	→	ladies		knife	→	knives
toy	→	toys		person	→	people

We don't use *a* or *an* before a plural noun. We can use the word *some* in an affirmative sentence and the word *any* in a question or a negative sentence.

*I've got **a** cake.*	→	*We've got **some** cakes.*
*Has he got **any** brothers?*	→	*No, he hasn't got **any** brothers.*

Notes

When we offer or ask for something, we use the word *some*, not *any*.
*Would you like **some** honey?*
*Can I have **some** biscuits, please?*

Uncountable nouns

There are other nouns which are uncountable. They do not have a plural form.

fruit	money	news	milk	furniture
homework	knowledge	water	equipment	rubbish
information	cheese	weather	time	chocolate
salt	music	progress	food	luggage

Would you like some fruit and some water?

I'd like some fruit, but I don't need any water, thanks. I've got some juice.

All uncountable nouns are followed by a singular verb.
*This music **is** lovely.*

We don't use *a* or *an* with uncountable nouns. We can use the word *some* in affirmative sentences and the word *any* in questions and negative sentences.
*I would like **some** water, please.*
*Have you got **any** money with you? No, I haven**'t** got **any** money.*

When we offer or ask for something, we usually use the word ***some***, not ***any***.
*Would you like **some** more pepper?*
*Could I have **some** milk, please?*

We can 'count' uncountable nouns by using containers and measurements.

bread	*a loaf of bread*	*three loaves of bread*
coffee	*a cup of coffee*	*three cups of coffee*
cola	*a can of cola*	*three cans of cola*
jam	*a jar of jam*	*three jars of jam*
milk	*a carton of milk*	*three cartons of milk*
rice	*a bowl of rice*	*three bowls of rice*
soup	*a tin of soup*	*three tins of soup*
sugar	*a bag of sugar*	*three bags of sugar*
tea	*a packet of tea*	*three packets of tea*
water	*a glass of water*	*three glasses of water*

1 **Complete the sentences with *some* or *any*. There may be more than one possible answer.**

1 Have you bought _____*any*_____ fruit for the picnic?

2 I saw _____ money on the table – is it yours?

3 Would you like _____ milk with your coffee?

4 Are there _____ biscuits in the cupboard?

5 Can you give me _____ information about trains to Warsaw, please?

6 Is there _____ rubbish to go in the bin?

7 We haven't had _____ news about grandma from the hospital today.

8 Do you want _____ food or just a glass of water?

9 Are there _____ bottles of water in the fridge?

10 There isn't _____ furniture in Sue's new flat.

2 **Tick (✓) the correct sentence, *a* or *b*.**

1 a There isn't some good music on the radio at the moment. ___
   b There isn't any good music on the radio at the moment. ✔

2 a He made good progresses at school this year. ___
   b He made good progress at school this year ___

3 a There isn't any traffic on the motorway. ___
   b There isn't some traffic on the motorway. ___

4 a Can I have any ketchup on my sandwich? ___
   b Can I have some ketchup on my sandwich? ___

5 a Have you got any milk? ___
   b Have you got some milk? ___

6 a He's got some luggage for his journey. ___
   b He's got any luggage for his journey. ___

7 a Would you like some fruit after the meal? ___
   b Would you like some fruits after the meal? ___

8 a Please buy two breads from the baker's. ___
   b Please buy two loaves of bread from the baker's. ___

Quantifiers: *a little/a few/a lot of*

We use *a little* with uncountable nouns to say that a small amount of something exists.
*There's only **a little** milk left in my glass.*

We use *a few* with plural countable nouns to say that a small number of something exists.
We can use *of* with *a few*.
*There are **a few** people waiting for the train.*
***A few of** my friends will be coming to the party.*

We use *a lot of* with uncountable and plural countable nouns. We usually use it in affirmative sentences.
*She's got **a lot of** luggage to carry.*
*There are **a lot of** interesting books in the library.*

3 **Circle the correct answer.**

1 There were ___ good reports on the news this evening.

  a little   b any   c⃝ a few

2 There might be ___ rain later on today.

  a few   b a lot   c a little

3 He'll need ___ luck if he's going to pass his English exam!

  a a lot of   b a few   c little

4 Will you put ___ salt in the soup?

  a few   b some   c little

5 We need ___ cups of coffee.

  a three   b a little   c any

6 Were there ___ people at the concert?

  a a lot of   b little   c a few

7 We still have ___ time left.

  a little   b a lot of   c a few

8 Please get ___ cans of cola while you're at the shop.

  a little   b some of   c a few

Much/many and not enough

We use *much* with uncountable nouns in negative sentences and questions.
*I haven't got **much** information about computers.*
*Is there much **money** in your bank account?*

We use *many* with plural countable nouns. We usually use it in negative sentences and questions.
*There aren't **many** biscuits left.*
*Were there **many** people on the bus this morning?*

We use *too much* with uncountable nouns and *too many* with plural countable nouns to talk about a quantity that is more than we need or want.
*There's **too much** rubbish on the streets.*
*There are **too many** people who throw rubbish in the streets.*

We use *not enough* with both uncountable nouns and plural countable nouns to talk about a quantity that is less than we need or want.
*I don't have **enough** money to buy that bicycle.*
*There **aren't enough** places for us to go in this town.*

4 **Complete the sentences with *much, many* or *not enough*.**

1 How _____ many _____ bags can we take on the plane?

2 There are _____ chairs for everyone to sit on.

3 She hasn't got _____ clothes.

4 I can't pay for your cola because I haven't got _____ money.

5 He's got too _____ homework to do tonight.

6 There are too _____ rules in English grammar!

7 There is _____ time to finish the test.

8 He hasn't made _____ progress in maths this term.

9 You paid too _____ money for those trainers.

10 Is there _____ rubbish outside?

Think about it!

We use *much* with uncountable nouns and *many* with countable nouns. We use *not enough* with both!

Both/either/neither/all/none

We use *both, either* and *neither* to talk about two people or things.
Both means *one and the other*.
Both of them go to that school.
He likes **both** rock and reggae music.

Either means *one or the other*.
I don't think **either** of the children go to that school.
I listen to **either** rock or reggae music.

Neither means *not one and not the other*.
Neither of the boys goes to that school.
His sister enjoys **neither** rock nor reggae music.

We use *all* and *none* to talk about more than two people or things. *All* means *every one of them*. *None* means *not even one of them*.
All the students in my class passed their final exam.
None of my friends play chess.

5 **Circle the correct answer.**

1 You can have *neither* / (*either*) the spaghetti or the pizza.

2 *All* / *Either* of the people I met at dance school last year are talented.

3 I'm not sure who broke the window. It was *either* / *both* Paul or John.

4 Put *all* / *none* the pictures on the wall – they'll look nice.

5 *None* / *Either* of the people in my family can speak Italian.

6 My friend and I are *either* / *neither* going to the beach or the mountains next summer.

7 *Neither* / *All* of my parents wants to live anywhere except our town.

8 *None* / *Neither* of the football fans were happy with the result.

9 They are *neither* / *all* going to help with the washing up.

10 Stop talking, *none* / *all* of you!

6 **Complete the sentences with the words from the box.**

> a lot of   both   either   enough   many   much   neither   none

1 We had _____a lot of_____ fun on the beach yesterday.
2 There isn't _____ cola. We can't all have a glass.
3 You can have _____ cake or ice cream for dessert.
4 I think he put too _____ vegetables in the soup.
5 My mum and dad are _____ good skiers. They love it!
6 _____ of the people in my English class have ever been to London.
7 I don't think there are _____ people who can run a marathon.
8 _____ I nor my brother understands Japanese.

Articles

The indefinite article – a/an

We use the indefinite article with:

- singular countable nouns that we talk about for the first time.
  *I can see **a** red Ferrari.*

- nouns that talk about someone's job or nationality.
  *He's **a** computer programmer.*
  *Is she **an** American?*

- certain numbers instead of *one* and in some quantifying phrases.
  ***a** hundred*
  ***a** million*
  *once **a** week*
  *50 km **an** hour*

We do not use the indefinite article with:

- plural countable nouns.
  Ferraris are great cars.

- uncountable nouns.
  There is cheese in the fridge.

- adjectives that are not followed by a noun.
  *He's nasty. (He's **a** nasty man.)*

- names of meals (except when there is an adjective before them).
  When do you want breakfast?
  *Let's have **a** cooked breakfast.*

7 **Complete the sentences with *a*, *an* or – .**

1 I'm sure that man is _____a_____ doctor.
2 I've got _____ hundred things to do.
3 You can't drive faster than 80 km _____ hour on this road.
4 That was _____ great party, thank you.
5 What _____ nice hair she's got!
6 What are we having for _____ dinner tonight?
7 Is your mum _____ scientist?
8 It's good for you to eat _____ apple every day.

Articles

The definite article – *the*

We use the definite article:

- with singular and plural countable nouns and with uncountable nouns.
  The cake is finished.
  The cakes are finished.
  The coffee is delicious.

- when we talk about someone or something that has been mentioned in a previous sentence.
  I met a man and a woman at a party.
  The man was friendly, but the woman wasn't.

- when we talk about someone or something specific.
  The girl with the red dress is my best friend.

- with nouns which are thought of as being unique.
  The Earth goes round the sun.

- with names of seas (*the Red Sea*), rivers (*the Amazon*), mountain ranges (*the Himalayas*), oceans (*the Pacific Ocean*) and deserts (*the Sahara*).

- with names of hotels (*the Holiday Inn*), theatres (*the Globe Theatre*), cinemas (*the Odeon Cinema*), ships (*the Titanic*), newspapers (*the Express*) and organisations (*the World Wildlife Fund*).

We do not use the definite article with:

- plural countable nouns when we talk in general.
  Lions are hunters.

- names of people, roads, cities, islands, countries or continents.
  His name is Dacso.
  I live in Prince's Street.
  Aliz is in Prague this week.
  Have you ever been to Barbados?
  I've never been to India.
  Europe is a big continent.

- abstract nouns.
  Love is a wonderful thing.

- with groups of islands and countries in the plural.
  We had a wonderful time in the Canary Islands last summer.
  I studied in the United States of America.

- with nationalities, musical instruments and family names.
  The Chinese eat with chopsticks.
  I'm learning to play the guitar.
  Do you know the Browns?

- with titles of people (without names).
  Who is the captain of this team?

- with the superlative form of adjectives.
  She's the cleverest girl in the class.
  He's the most interesting person I know.

- with numbers showing frequency and the words *last* and *only*.
  That's the third time he's been late for school this week.
  This is the last thing to go in the suitcase.
  He's the only boy in the dance class.

- with dates and the words *morning*, *afternoon* and *evening*.
  I'm getting married on 5th September.
  (We say the fifth of September.)
  I'll go to the supermarket in the afternoon.

- the words *hospital, church, bed, home, prison, work* and *school*.
  What time will you be home tonight?

- names of meals.
  What shall we have for dinner?

- names of languages when we don't say the word *language*.
  Japanese is very difficult.
  The Japanese language is very difficult.

- titles of people when we say their name.
  Prince Charles is the father of Prince William.

8 **Complete the sentences with *the* or –.**

1   Have you read a lot about _____the_____ ancient Greeks?

2   How many of _____ Caribbean Islands have you been to?

3   _____ beauty is not as important as brains.

4   My father plays _____ guitar.

5   They went to _____ Grand Canyon when they visited _____ USA.

6   _____ Sheraton Hotel is in _____ Regent Street.

7   We're inviting _____ Greens and _____ John and Freda Williams to the party.

8   Where are we going after _____ lunch?

9   Do you speak _____ French?

10 **Find the mistakes in the sentences. Then write them correctly.**

1   Do you know where a Queen's Hotel is?
    _Do you know where the Queen's Hotel is?_____

2   Dad is still in the bed.
    _____
    _____

3   Are you enjoying studying the English?
    _____
    _____

4   They first met on holiday in Canary Islands.
    _____
    _____

5   Was your grandfather the doctor?
    _____
    _____

6   Police officer is searching for clues.
    _____
    _____

7   Prime Minister made a speech.
    _____
    _____

8   The giraffes have very long necks.
    _____
    _____

9 **Complete the sentences with *a, an* or *the*.**

1   How long has he lived in _____the_____ Middle East?

2   Have you seen _____ girl who owns that coat?

3   I think I want _____ sandwich and _____ drink now.

4   Where is _____ park you went to last Saturday?

5   Astronauts are hoping to walk on _____ moon before long.

6   Have you got _____ pen I could borrow, please?

7   I'd hate to be left in _____ Arizona Desert without any water!

8   I'll have _____ orange instead of cake for my dessert.

11 **Find the extra word and write it in the space.**

1   You've got the beautiful eyes!
    _____the_____

2   Please be quiet. I've got a homework to do.
    _____

3   The criminal will stay in the prison for a very long time. _____

4   He's the only boy I know who can to play the violin. _____

5   We have to go to a school every day during term time. _____

6   Do you like the cats as pets? _____

7   I spent my holidays in the France.
    _____

8   Do you want a milk in your cereal?
    _____

12 **Complete the text with *a*, *an*, *the* or –.**

On Monday, we had [1] _____an_____ English lesson with [2] _____ Mrs Green.
[3] _____ lesson is usually on [4] _____ Friday, but she was ill last week. She told
us all about [5] _____ London and [6] _____ England, where she went last year
for her summer holidays. She speaks very good [7] _____ English, so she had no trouble
talking to people and getting around. It was [8] _____ second time she had been there and
she said that it was [9] _____ best holiday she had ever had.

She stayed at [10] _____ Kensington Hotel, she went to [11] _____ Royal
Palace Theatre and she took [12] _____ boat trip on [13] _____ River Thames.
[14] _____ most interesting thing about her trip was the day she visited Buckingham Palace.
She didn't see [15] _____ Queen though!

During the second week of her holiday, she went on a day trip to [16] _____ France.
She was scared of going through the Channel Tunnel, so she took [17] _____ ferry across
[18] _____ English Channel instead.

This year she isn't going to [19] _____ England. She's going to Greece and she's going to
visit some of [20] _____ Ionian Islands.

Pairwork

Look inside your bag and talk to your partner about what is inside it.

For example:

There is a pen and some pencils.

The pen is blue and the pencils are black.

There are some books.

Writing

Write a short paragraph describing your bedroom. Try to use as many of the words from the box as possible.

a	a few	a little	all	a lot of	an	any	both	either
not enough	many	much	neither	none	some	the		

In my bedroom there is a bed and a desk. Both of them are made of wood. There are some bookshelves near the bed.

Future perfect simple

Affirmative	Negative	Question
I will (I'll) have answered	I will not (won't) have answered	Will I have answered?
you will (you'll) have answered	you will not (won't) have answered	Will you have answered?
he will (he'll) have answered	he will not (won't) have answered	Will he have answered?
she will (she'll) have answered	she will not (won't) have answered	Will she have answered?
it will (it'll) have answered	it will not (won't) have answered	Will it have answered?
we will (we'll) have answered	we will not (won't) have answered	Will we have answered?
you will (you'll) have answered	you will not (won't) have answered	Will you have answered?
they will (they'll) have answered	they will not (won't) have answered	Will they have answered?

Short answers

Yes, I/you will.	No, I won't.
Yes, he/she/it will.	No, you won't.
Yes, we/you/they will.	No, he/she/it won't.
	No, we/you/they won't.

We use the future perfect simple to talk about something that will be complete before something else happens or before a specific time in the future.

(It's five o'clock and I'm doing my homework. I will be doing my homework for another hour and a half.)
*By seven o'clock, I **will have finished** my homework.*
(It's already 9 p.m. Panit still has a lot of pages to read.)
*Panit **won't have finished** his book before he goes to bed.*

Are you still doing your homework?

Yes, but by supper time, I'll have finished all of it. I'll have answered fifty questions!

1 Complete the sentences with the future perfect simple.

1 They _____will have made_____ (make) their beds before they have breakfast.

2 She _____ (have) a shower before she goes to school.

3 I _____ (finish) this book before I go to bed tonight.

4 It _____ (snow) at least once before next summer.

5 You _____ (write) more than fifty essays before you leave school.

6 We _____ (ride) 40 km before it gets dark.

7 He _____ (send) all his friends text messages before tomorrow morning.

8 Mum _____ (go) to work before I get up tomorrow.

Think about it!

Like other future tenses, the form of the future perfect simple is the same for every person: *will* + *have* + past participle.

2 Rewrite the sentences as questions.

1 Doctors will have found a cure for cancer before the 22nd century.

 Will doctors have found a cure for cancer
 before the 22nd century?

2 Astronauts will have walked on Mars before the end of this century.

 _____

 _____

3 Monkeys will have learnt how to use computers before the year 2040.

 _____

 _____

4 He will have travelled to India before he goes to university.

 _____

 _____

5 The firefighters will have put out the forest fire before it gets dark tonight.

 _____

 _____

3 Write negative sentences.

1 he / earn / enough money / for a new car / before he's twenty

 He won't have earned enough money for a
 new car before he's twenty.

2 they / study / before their exam

 _____

 _____

3 her baby / learn / how to talk / before it's three months old

 _____

 _____

4 she / make / the dinner / before four o'clock

 _____

 _____

5 you / drink / all that milk / before you go to bed

 _____

 _____

6 we / eat / dinner / before we go out

 _____

 _____

Time expressions with the future perfect

before ...	by the time ...	in ten minutes
by five o'clock	by Wednesday	soon
by next week	by the weekend	
by now	in a year's time	

4 **Complete the sentences with *by* or *in*.**

1 He will have lived here for ten years _____ by _____ next summer.

2 I will have left school _____ two years.

3 _____ this evening, she will have learnt all her English grammar.

4 They will have finished their dinner _____ half an hour.

5 The doctor will have examined twenty patients _____ the time she leaves work.

6 I think I will have passed all my exams _____ the end of the year.

7 She won't have done all her homework _____ an hour.

8 Will he have phoned you _____ the weekend?

5 **Complete the sentences with the verbs from the box. Use the future perfect.**

cook discover finish have learn start (x2) win

1 He _____ will have started _____ a new school by next month.

2 _____ you _____ how to play the violin by next summer?

3 Scientists _____ new ways of making energy by the year 2050.

4 The chef _____ more unusual recipes by this time next year.

5 The athlete _____ more medals by the end of the competition.

6 The film _____ by the time you arrive. Don't come to the cinema.

7 I _____ another birthday by this time next year.

8 His computer course _____ by the end of August.

Think about it!

In order to be good at the future perfect simple you have to know the past participles of irregular verbs very well. Use the list on page 198 to learn them.

6 **Write the words in the correct order.**

1 have / you / your house / will / by December / built / ?

    Will you have built your house by December?

2 had / go out / I / before / will / a bath / I / have

    _____

    _____

3 have / won't / he / before / finished / to school / goes / his homework / he

    _____

    _____

4 before / will / snowed / tomorrow / wake up / we / it / have / ?

    _____

    _____

5 have / his presents / he / will / opened / his birthday / before / ?

    _____

    _____

6 the students / have / their new teacher / by this afternoon / will / met

    _____

    _____

7 will / by next year / have / they / got married / ?

    _____

    _____

8 you / made / by the time / she arrives / have / will / lunch

    _____

    _____

7 Match 1–6 with a–f.

1	I will have read	a	at school for a couple of months by November?
2	Will you have been	b	their breakfast by nine o'clock?
3	They won't have seen	c	each other for three years next month.
4	She'll have seen	d	four books by Saturday.
5	Will they have eaten	e	my homework by tomorrow.
6	I won't have finished	f	her new teacher before she leaves school today.

8 Tick (✔) the correct sentence, *a* or *b*.

1   a   We will have moved to another city until next year. ___
    b   We will have moved to another city by next year. ✔

2   a   You will have forgotten me by the time you're thirty? ___
    b   Will you have forgotten me by the time you're thirty? ___

3   a   They won't have eaten supper before eight o'clock. ___
    b   They won't eaten supper before eight o'clock. ___

4   a   This film won't have finish by the time I go to bed. ___
    b   This film won't have finished by the time I go to bed. ___

5   a   She will have learnt Spanish by the time she is twenty. ___
    b   She will have learnt Spanish before the time she is twenty. ___

6   a   He will have bought a shirt before the party on Saturday. ___
    b   He will have bought a shirt at the party on Saturday. ___

9 Complete the sentences with the future perfect simple.

1   I'm writing an essay. I'll finish at a quarter to six.
    By nine o'clock _____ I'll have written _____ (write) an essay.

2   They're listening to a podcast. They'll finish in half an hour.
    In forty minutes, _____ (listen) to a podcast.

3   She's having a shower. She'll finish at half past seven.
    By eight o'clock, _____ (have) a shower.

4   We're eating dinner. We'll finish at half past nine.
    By ten o'clock, _____ (eat) dinner.

5   It's raining. It will stop before it gets dark.
    By the time it gets dark, _____ (stop) raining.

6   I'm doing my homework. I'll finish at seven o'clock.
    By half past seven, _____ (do) my homework.

10 **Write affirmative sentences with the future perfect.**

SIMON'S JOBS FOR TODAY

make my bed

read an English magazine

finish tidying my bedroom

wash my black T-shirt

buy a present for Mum

do my homework

go for a walk

bake Mum's birthday cake

1 Simon will have made his bed.

2 _____

3 _____

4 _____

5 _____

6 _____

7 _____

8 _____

11 **Find the mistakes in the sentences. Then write them correctly.**

1 What will you <u>had</u> studied before you go to bed tonight?

   What will you have studied before you go to bed tonight?

2 Will you have learn to drive by the time you're twenty?

   _____

3 Which countries have you will visited by the time you're thirty?

   _____

4 She will haven't seen the pyramids before she returns from Egypt.

   _____

5 They won't has given away all their toys by the time they're thirteen.

   _____

6 That family will have leaved London before the end of the year.

   _____

7 Until the end of the year, she will have passed her exams.

   _____

8 He won't haven't finished the cleaning by the end of the day.

   _____

12 **Find the extra word and write it in the space.**

1 What will you have <u>will</u> done before you meet me at the weekend? _____will_____

2 Do you think the weather it will have got worse before we arrive? _____

3 I will have to lived in this house for thirteen years by next April. _____

4 They won't not have saved a lot of money by the end of the month. _____

5 Will he have and got his degree by the time he's 23? _____

6 Who will have been visited your house by this time next week? _____

7 By until tomorrow morning, she will have got better. _____

8 He will have been finished his homework by eight o'clock. _____

13 **Complete the text by writing one word in each gap.**

I wonder what I will [1]_____have_____ done before the end of the week. I imagine
I [2]_____ have eaten quite a lot of food, and I will have [3]_____ a lot of milk
and juice. I will [4]_____ slept for at least forty hours [5]_____ the end of the
week and [6]_____ will have spent about thirty hours in lessons. I will have spoken
[7]_____ a lot of people and I'll [8]_____ watched a lot of programmes on TV.
I think I will have improved my English grammar by the end of the week. I hope
I [9]_____ have learnt some new things and maybe have [10]_____ some new
friends. I think I will have been very busy by the time the week ends!

Pairwork

Work in pairs. Take turns to tell each other as many things as possible that you will have done before you see each other again.

Writing

Write an email to your friend telling them all the things you think you will have done in ten years' time. Think about the points below.

- your home
- your family
- your holidays and free time
- your studies/job
- your friends

1 Circle the correct answer.

1   Where ___ stay when you're on holiday in Italy?

   a   you   (b)   are you going to   c   will you being

2   Do you think Dad ___ give me a lift to the coffee shop later?

   a   is going to   b   will being   c   will

3   My favourite rock group ___ in a concert in London next month.

   a   performs   b   is performing   c   will perform

4   We're not going ___ any more time playing computer games!

   a   wasting   b   to waste   c   waste

5   Natasha ___ her grandparents next weekend.

   a   is visiting   b   is going   c   will to visit

6   What time does your flight ___ in the morning?

   a   is taking off   b   will take off   c   take off

7   ___ work until nine o'clock tomorrow evening?

   a   Is he going to   b   Will he to   c   Does he

8   ___ we have another ice-cream?

   a   Shall   b   Will   c   Having

2 Find the mistakes in the sentences. Then write them correctly.

1   Mum and Dad buy a new fridge next month.

   Mum and Dad are going to buy a new fridge next month.

2   Are you going spend the weekend with your best friend?

   _____

   _____

3   Does this train leaves at five o'clock or six o'clock?

   _____

   _____

4   I'll seeing you tomorrow.

   _____

   _____

5   Thomas is play in the basketball finals on Saturday.

   _____

   _____

6   I'm going to not talk to Laura ever again!

   _____

   _____

7   Do you come to the supermarket with me tomorrow morning?

   _____

   _____

8   I'm sure it does be hot tomorrow.

   _____

   _____

3 Complete the sentences with the present continuous, present simple or future simple.

1   I ___am having___ (have) a party at the weekend. Do you want to come?

2   I promise I _____ (be) home before it gets dark.

3   He _____ (take) his English exam next month.

4   The train from Budapest _____ (arrive) at half past two.

5   I know you _____ (enjoy) the film that's on TV tonight.

6   We _____ (eat out) tomorrow evening. Dad's already booked a table.

7   The plane to Cairo _____ (take off) at ten o'clock.

8   I _____ (carry) that bag for you. It looks heavy.

4 **Complete the sentences with the future continuous or future simple.**

1 The reporter _____ will be talking _____ (talk) about his visit to China in tonight's documentary.

2 My sister _____ (sleep) when I get home tonight.

3 I am sure he _____ (win) the race.

4 I'm so tired that I think I _____ (go) to bed straight away.

5 The judge _____ (make) his decision in two hours.

6 I promise I _____ (never lie) to you again!

7 Our local cinema _____ (show) comedy films on Saturday night.

8 _____ (we / buy) these video games?

5 **Find the extra word and write it in the space.**

1 Where will you <u>are</u> be going after the party? _____ are _____

2 I'm sure it will be being foggy later this evening. _____

3 I don't know what will be happen if I fail this exam! _____

4 I wonder how much we'll be to paying for clothes in 2030. _____

5 How often will you be visit your parents if you go to live in England? _____

6 Will you write to me when will I go? _____

7 I'll feel be feeling nervous before my exam tomorrow. _____

8 What you will you be thinking about when you wake up in the morning? _____

6 **Circle the correct answer.**

1 I promise I ___ you a postcard from Scotland.

  (a) will send   b will be sending   c do send

2 I wonder if it ___ tomorrow morning when I wake up.

  a will raining   b is raining   c will be raining

3 Who ___ for you at the airport when you arrive?

  a will wait   b will be   c will be waiting

4 What ___ this time tomorrow?

  a will you do   b will you be doing   c you will be doing

5 ___ ever see him again?

  a You will   b Will you being   c Will you

6 Who do you think ___ the President of the USA in 2030?

  a will be   b will   c will being

7 Will people still ___ meat in 2025?

  a eating   b will eat   c be eating

8 Who ___ your breakfast for you in five years' time?

  a will be making   b makes   c will be make

7 **Find the mistakes in the sentences. Then write them correctly.**

1   I've got some relations who live in <u>the</u> Wales.
    <u>I've got some relations who live in Wales.</u>

2   What is the name of Prime Minister of Greece?
    _____

3   I didn't know Jacobsen's were your neighbours.
    _____

4   Did you stay in a Regency Hotel in Thailand?
    _____

5   She thinks Akeem has got the beautiful eyes.
    _____

6   Have you seen a dress I bought?
    _____

7   My grandfather is at supermarket at the moment.
    _____

8   It's one o'clock. Shall we have the lunch?
    _____

9   The River Thames is in the London.
    _____

10 The people should protect the environment we live in.
    _____

8 **Circle the correct answer.**

1   Have you got ___ books to lend me?
    a   a little   (b) a few   c   a lot

2   We saw ___ unusual animals when we went to the zoo.
    a   a little of   b   a few of   c   a lot of

3   I think we should ___ go to the cinema or the bowling alley.
    a   neither   b   both   c   either

4   We still have ___ time left. If we hurry, we might catch the train.
    a   a little   b   much   c   a few

5   There isn't ___ cheese on this pizza.
    a   many   b   either   c   much

6   Are ___ the students in your English class as good as you are?
    a   either   b   all   c   none

7   I don't think we bought ___ juice for the party.
    a   too   b   not enough   c   enough

8   There are ___ books on this shelf. It will break.
    a   too many   b   too much   c   not enough

9 **Complete the sentences with *some* or *any*. There may be more than one possible answer.**

1   Can I have _____ <u>some</u> _____ money to go shopping?

2   We saw _____ interesting paintings in the art gallery.

3   I haven't got _____ nice clothes to wear to the party.

4   Have you got _____ time to explain this to me?

5   There's isn't _____ milk left, so we can't have a milkshake.

6   There are _____ great sights to see in London.

7   Are there _____ good museums in your town?

8   Would you like _____ apple juice?

10 **Complete the sentences with the future perfect simple.**

1 They ____will not have finished____ (not finish) all this homework by eleven o'clock tonight.

2 He _____ (apologise) to Mum for being rude by the time Dad gets home.

3 _____ you _____ (eat) your supper before eight o'clock this evening?

4 Those students _____ (not write) their essays before the next lesson.

5 She _____ (leave) this school before her sister starts here.

6 _____ you _____ (send) him an email by this time tomorrow?

7 Do you think it _____ (rain) by the time we get up in the morning?

8 I'm sure she _____ (make) enough sandwiches for the party.

11 **Complete the sentences with *by* or *in*.**

1 I will have done all my homework _____by_____ the end of today.

2 _____ a year's time, I'll have learnt how to play the piano.

3 Will you have learnt how to use your new laptop _____ the time we go on holiday?

4 He won't have arrived _____ eight o'clock.

5 We will have moved to a new house _____ next September.

6 They will have come back from town _____ an hour.

7 He won't have finished that book _____ this afternoon.

8 _____ half an hour, the sun will have come up.

12 **Find the mistakes in the sentences. Then write them correctly.**

1 Will you have phoned him <u>for</u> the time we go out tonight?

   <u>Will you have phoned him by the time we go out tonight?</u>

2 My mother won't have been done all her jobs by tonight.

   _____

3 In ten o'clock this evening, they will have listened to a hundred songs.

   _____

4 I think computers they will have changed a lot by the year 2050.

   _____

5 We will had set off on our journey before the sun rises.

   _____

6 In the end of October, he'll have been at that school for a year.

   _____

7 How much bread will she have been selling by lunchtime?

   _____

8 Mum will have go to bed before we get home.

   _____

Can/could/be able to and must/have to

Affirmative	Negative	Question
I/you can write	I/you cannot (can't) write	Can I/you write?
he/she/it can write	he/she/it cannot (can't) write	Can he/she/it write?
we/you/they can write	we/you/they cannot (can't) write	Can we/you/they write?

Short answers

Yes, I/you can.	No, I/you can't.
Yes, he/she/it can.	No, he/she/it can't.
Yes, we/you/they can.	No, we/you/they can't.

We use *can*:

- to talk about ability in the present.
  *She **can** ride a horse.*
  *He **can't** speak Italian.*

- to talk about or ask for permission.
  ***Can** I have some more chocolate?*
  *No, you **can't**!*

- to make requests.
  ***Can** you bring me a glass of water, please?*

Notes

Even though we don't use *can* in the future simple (we use *will be able to*), when we talk about present decisions concerning future ability, we *use can*.
*We **can't** finish our project today, but we **can** finish it tomorrow morning.*

We use *can* in a negative question when we want to show that we are surprised or upset by something.
***Can't** you come to my party at the weekend?*

I wrote this song! Do you like it?

It's amazing! I can't write songs, but I would love to be able to!

1 **Complete the sentences with *can* and the words in brackets.**

1 _____Can you speak_____ (you / speak) French?

2 We _____ (not hear) what he is saying.

3 _____ (I / have) some money to go shopping, please?

4 They _____ (not come) out with us on Saturday because their mum is ill.

5 _____ (he / play) the guitar?

6 You _____ (not open) the cupboard because it is locked.

7 We _____ (not go) into the staff room.

8 _____ (I / have) a glass of milk, please?

9 _____ (you / turn) the light on, please?

10 I _____ (not see)! It's too dark in here.

Think about it!

We only use *cannot* instead of *can't* in very formal writing or speaking. In normal everyday language, we use *can't*.

Could

Affirmative	Negative	Question
I/you could write	I/you could not (couldn't) write	Could I/you write?
he/she/it could write	he/she/it could not (couldn't) write	Could he/she/it write?
we/you/they could write	we/you/they could not (couldn't) write	Could we/you/they write?

Short answers	
Yes, I/you could.	No, I/you couldn't.
Yes, he/she/it could.	No, he/she/it couldn't.
Yes, we/you/they could.	No, we/you/they couldn't.

We use *could*:

- to talk about past ability.
  *He **could** ride a bike when he was four.*

- to ask for permission in the present and future.
  ***Could** I borrow your pen, please?*
  ***Could** I stay at home on Monday?*

- to make a polite request.
  ***Could** you open the door for me, please?*

Notes

We do not use *could* for ability in the past to talk about one specific time when we managed to do something. In this case, we must use *was/were able to*.
*She **was able to** post my letter for me yesterday.*

2 **Write questions with the verb in brackets.**

1 borrow some money please (can)
  Can I borrow some money, please?

2 have a glass of water (could)
  _____

3 pass me the wooden spoon (could)
  _____

4 use your bike today (can)
  _____

5 tell me the time (could)
  _____

6 use your computer (can)
  _____

Be able to

Affirmative	Negative	Question
I am (I'm) able to write	I am not (I'm not) able to write	Am I able to write?
you are (you're) able to write	you are not (aren't) able to write	Are you able to write?
he/she/it is (he's/she's/it's) able to write	he/she/it is not (isn't) able to write	Is he/she/it able to write?
we/you/they are (we're/you're/they're) able to write	we/you/they are not (aren't) able to write	Are we/you/they able to write?

Short answers	
Yes, I am.	No, I'm not.
Yes, you are.	No, you aren't.
Yes, he/she/it is.	No, he/she/it isn't.
Yes, we/you/they are.	No, we/you/they aren't.

Be able to can be used in a number of tenses. It is not used in continuous tenses.

Present simple – *I **am able to**, you **are able to**,* etc.
Past simple – *I **was able to**, you **were able to**,* etc.
Present perfect simple – *I **have been able to**, you **have been able to**,* etc.
Past perfect simple – *I **had been able to**, you **had been able to**,* etc.
Future simple – *I **will be able to**, you **will be able to**,* etc.

We use *be able to*:

• to talk about ability.
  *We **are able to** see the sea from our house.*
  *He'll **be able to** go to school tomorrow.*

• to talk about a specific occasion when we managed (or didn't manage) to do something.
  *I **was able to** help him with his homework last night.* (We cannot use *could* here.)
  *I **wasn't able to** help him with his homework last night.* (We can use *couldn't* here.)

Notes
With verbs of the senses, we use *could* and not *be able to*.
*We **could** hear the thunder in the distance.*
*She **could** see that Martin was upset.*

3 **Complete the sentences with the correct form of *be able to* and the words in brackets.**

1 _____ Were you able to guess _____ (you / guess) the answers in yesterday's test?
2 _____ (you / help) me with my homework tomorrow?
3 He _____ (never understand) maths when he was at school.
4 _____ (she / play) the piano?
5 Tom lost his keys yesterday and he _____ (not find) them yet.
6 _____ (you / explain) the rules to the new student tomorrow?
7 Grandma _____ (not visit) us on Sunday because she wasn't feeling well.
8 Mika _____ (use) a computer from a very early age.

4 **Circle the correct answer.**

1 *Can you*/ *Are you able to* bring me my bag, please?

2 When she was ten, she *was able to* / *can* speak three languages.

3 As soon as I got home, I *can* / *could* smell something very nice cooking.

4 He *wasn't able to* / *can't* ride the horse and he fell off.

5 *Am I able to* / *Can I* go out for a minute?

6 Why *you couldn't* / *can't you* keep your room tidy?

7 She *couldn't* / *isn't able to* play the piano last year, but now she can.

8 I hope I'll *can* / *be able to* pass all my exams next year.

9 They *can't* / *weren't able to* speak English when they were three years old.

10 She *could* / *is able to* drive a car now because she passed her driving test last month.

11 You *can* / *are be able to* finish your essay tomorrow if you want.

12 The cat was locked in, but it *was able to* / *could* escape through the window.

Mustn't

Affirmative	Negative	Question
I/you must write he/she/it must write we/you/they must write	I/you must not (mustn't) write he/she/it must not (mustn't) write we/you/they must not (mustn't) write	Must I/you write? Must he/she/it write? Must we/you/they write?

Short answers	
Yes, I/you must.	No, I/you mustn't.
Yes, he/she/it must.	No, he/she/it mustn't.
Yes, we/you/they must.	No, we/you/they mustn't.

We use *must*:

- to talk about obligation.
  *You **must follow** the diet the doctor gave you.*

- to talk about necessity.
  *I'm sorry, but we **must go** now.*

We use *mustn't*:

- to talk about prohibition.
  *You **mustn't eat** in class.*

Notes

We do not usually use *must* in the question form.

5 **Complete the sentences with *could, couldn't, must* or *mustn't*.**

1   Before you get on the plane at the airport,
    you _____*must*_____ show your passport.

2   You _____ use bad language.

3   The fire alarm has gone off. We
    _____ leave the building.

4   Jenny _____ find her glasses
    this morning.

5   _____ you tell me the way to
    the library, please?

6   Galina _____ never understand
    why he was angry.

7   We _____ remember where
    Mum had parked the car.

8   They _____ give back what
    they took immediately!

Have to/don't have to

Affirmative	Negative	Question
I/you have to write	I/you do not (don't) have to write	Do I/you have to write?
he/she/it has to write	he/she/it does not (doesn't) have to write	Does he/she/it have to write?
we/you/they have to write	we/you/they do not (don't) have to write	Do we/you/they have to write?

Short answers	
Yes, I/you do.	No, I/you don't.
Yes, he/she/it does.	No, he/she/it doesn't.
Yes, we/you/they do.	No, we/you/they don't.

Have to can be used in a number of tenses. We do not usually use it in continuous tenses.

Present simple – *I **have to**, you **have to***, etc.
Past simple – *I **had to**, you **had to***, etc.
Present perfect simple – *I **have had to**, you **have had to***, etc.
Past perfect simple – *I **had had to**, you **had had to***, etc.
Future simple – *I **will have to**, you **will have to***, etc.

We use *have to* to talk about obligation.
*I **have to** go to a piano lesson tomorrow.*

We use *don't have to* to talk about something that is not a necessity.
*I **don't have to** finish my homework this evening because it is Saturday tomorrow.*

We use the question form to ask if someone is obliged to do something.
***Do** I **have to** tidy my bedroom now?*
***Does** he **have to** take the rubbish out?*

6 Complete the sentences with the correct form of *have to* and the verbs from the box.

> apologise   be   do   get up   ~~go~~   make

1   Shura _____ has to go _____ to the dentist's.
2   _____ I _____ early every morning?
3   You _____ the washing up. I'll do it later.
4   He _____ his bed at the weekend, only during the week.
5   We _____ careful when we go on holiday next week. We don't want to get sunburnt.
6   Zikri _____ to the teacher because he was late again.

Must/have to and *mustn't/don't have to*

Must usually expresses internal obligation whereas *have to* expresses external obligation.
I **must** hurry or I'll miss the bus.
I **have to** tidy my room every day. (Because my mother tells me to.)

Mustn't and *don't have to* have completely different meanings.
You **mustn't** be late for the concert. (It's forbidden.)
You **don't have to** wear anything special to the party. (You can decide.)

---

7 Complete the sentences with the correct form of *must, mustn't, have to* or *don't have to* and the verb in brackets.

1   They _____ have to be _____ (be) at the school by 8 a.m. The teacher will be waiting!
2   She _____ (go) and see the doctor about her cough.
3   You _____ (take) those magazines out of the library.
4   He _____ (feed) the cat – I'll feed it later.
5   People _____ (leave) litter on the beach.
6   We _____ (remember) to buy a present for her birthday.
7   Those children are lucky; they _____ (wear) school uniforms.
8   I _____ (go) to football practice today because my trainer said I should have a rest.
9   Maria _____ (try) harder to improve her English.
10 We _____ (be) on time for our classes.

Think about it!

We also use *must* when we are giving strong advice.

8 **Rewrite the sentences using the word in bold. Use between two and five words.**

1 Is it necessary to write down so many words? **have**

Do we _____ have to write _____ down so many words?

2 I couldn't run very fast when I was little. **able**

I _____ run very fast when I was little.

3 Talking is not allowed in the exam room. **talk**

You _____ in the exam room.

4 She knows how to play the piano very well. **can**

She _____ the piano very well.

5 It's impossible for them to come next summer. **be**

They _____ come next summer.

6 Is it so difficult for you to sit down quietly and get on with your work? **can't**

_____ just sit down quietly and get on with your work?

9 **Tick (✔) the correct sentence, *a* or *b*.**

1 a They must take more exercise if they want to be fit. ✔

   b They must to take more exercise if they want to be fit. ___

2 a I must not go now – it is very late. ___

   b I must go now – it is very late. ___

3 a You mustn't to read the whole book, just the first chapter. ___

   b You don't have to read the whole book, just the first chapter. ___

4 a I won't be able come to the concert on Friday. ___

   b I won't be able to come to the concert on Friday. ___

5 a She didn't have to study last night, so she listened to music and read a magazine. ___

   b She didn't had to study last night, so she listened to music and read a magazine. ___

6 a Could you to finish quickly so we can go out? ___

   b Could you finish quickly so we can go out? ___

7 a She can't able to sing, but she acts really well. ___

   b She can't sing, but she acts really well. ___

8 a He must make an appointment at his dentist's. ___

   b He must to make an appointment at his dentist's. ___

10 **Complete the sentences in your own words.**

1   I mustn't _____ *forget to do my homework tonight* _____ .
2   You don't have to _____ .
3   Can you _____ ?
4   Will they be able to _____ ?
5   We have to _____ .
6   He couldn't _____ .

Pairwork

Work in pairs. Imagine that you are in control of a space station and that you are making the rules for the small society there. Discuss ten rules you would make. Use *must, mustn't, have to* and *don't have to*.

Writing

Write an email to a friend asking them if they can play any musical instruments, do any sports, speak any foreign languages, etc. Tell your friend what you can and can't do, and also what you could or couldn't do when you were younger.

Should, ought to, must, can't and may, might

Should/shouldn't for advice

Affirmative	Negative	Question
I/you should listen	I/you should not (shouldn't) listen	Should I/you listen?
he/she/it should listen	he/she/it should not (shouldn't) listen	Should he/she/it listen?
we/you/they should listen	we/you/they should not (shouldn't) listen	Should we/you/they listen?

Short answers	
Yes, I/you should.	No, I/you shouldn't.
Yes, he/she/it should.	No, he/she/it shouldn't.
Yes, we/you/they should.	No, we/you/they shouldn't.

We use *should*:

- to give advice.
  *I **should** get more exercise.*
  *You **shouldn't** eat so many sweets.*

- to ask for advice.
  ***Should** we buy Mum some flowers?*
  ***Should** we go and visit him in hospital?*

Should I open my present now or should I wait until my birthday?

1 **Complete the sentences with *should* or *shouldn't* and the verbs from the box.**

> book clean eat revise spend
> stay tell train ~~visit~~ worry

1 He ____should visit____ his grandparents more often.
2 _____ I _____ the neighbours that we're going to have a party?
3 You _____ out late because you have school tomorrow.
4 He _____ too many biscuits and cakes.
5 We _____ so many hours playing computer games.
6 The team _____ harder if they want to win the championship.
7 You _____ at the last minute for your test – you'll never remember everything!
8 _____ we _____ a table at the restaurant for Saturday evening?
9 You _____ about her – she'll be fine!
10 Pasha _____ his football boots – they're filthy!

Ought to/ought not to

Ought to/ought not to mean the same as *should/shouldn't*. We use them to give advice.
I **ought to** start doing my project.
You **ought to** pay attention in class.
He **ought to** see his doctor.
You **ought not to** fight with your brother.
She **ought not to** watch so much TV.
They **ought not to** play their music so loud.
I **ought to** eat more vegetables; they're good for me.
I **should** eat more vegetables; they're good for me.

Notes

We do not use *ought to* in the question form.

2 **Complete the sentences in your own words. Use *ought to* or *ought not to* and an appropriate verb.**

1 Young children ____ought not to watch____ too much television.
2 You _____ that letter today if you want it to get there by Friday.
3 We _____ her some flowers for her birthday.
4 They _____ their bikes to school instead of going by car.
5 You _____ more fish because it is very good for you.
6 Sally _____ so hard – she never relaxes at all.
7 I _____ another piece of cake, but it is really delicious!
8 He _____ home late tonight.
9 The girls _____ their bedroom at the weekend.
10 Amanda _____ so much money on video games.

3 **Write sentences with *should, shouldn't, ought to* or *ought not to*. There may be more than one possible answer.**

1 take jewellery to the beach

  You shouldn't take jewellery to the beach.

2 wear a sun hat and sunglasses when it's hot

  _____

  _____

3 put plenty of sun cream on if you go in the sun

  _____

  _____

4 eat a lot before you have a swim

  _____

5 swim in the deep end of the pool if you can't swim very well

  _____

  _____

6 throw sand when you're playing on the beach

  _____

  _____

Must/can't for deduction

We use *must* to say that we are sure something is true.
*That **must** be my friend at the door.* (I asked him to come over.)

We use *can't* to say that we are sure something is not true.
*That **can't** be the right phone number.* (I've tried ringing it several times.)

---

4 **Complete the sentences with *must be* or *can't be*.**

1 (The phone has just started to ring.)

  That _____must be_____ Sarah – she said she was going to phone this evening.

2 (You don't have your watch.)

  I wonder what time it is. It _____ late because the shops are still open.

3 (She said something bad about your friend, Tom.)

  She _____ right! He's always been very kind to me.

4 (Your best friend is playing tennis.)

  That _____ Martin on the phone. He's playing tennis.

5 (You are writing to a friend who lives in Canada.)

  What's the weather like there? It _____ very cold in the winter!

6 (A girl at your school has won a prize for her piano playing.)

  If she won a prize, then she _____ brilliant at playing the piano!

7 (Your brother has just eaten three doughnuts.)

  That _____ a record! Three doughnuts in two minutes!

8 (Your friend is showing you a photo of her mother.)

  That _____ your mother! She looks too young!

5 **Rewrite the sentences using the word in bold. Use between two and five words.**

1 It would be better for you to go to the doctor's. **should**

You _____should go_____ to the doctor's.

2 I'm sure that isn't John. He is in the library. **can't**

That _____ John. He is in the library.

3 Don't speak to your sister like that! **ought**

You _____ to your sister like that!

4 I know he is a thief. I saw him take the money. **must**

He _____ a thief. I saw him take the money.

5 Don't read in the dark; it is bad for your eyes. **shouldn't**

You _____ in the dark; it is bad for your eyes.

6 Fix the brakes on your bike or you will have an accident. **to**

You _____ the brakes on your
bike or you will have an accident.

May/might for possibility

We use *may* and *might* to say that something is a possibility.
I **might** go to the park on Saturday.
It **may** rain tomorrow.
We **might** have a picnic this afternoon.
You **may not** like the new teacher.
He **might not** come to school tomorrow.
They **may not** pass their exams.
It **may** rain later on.
We **might** be late because of the bad weather.

6 **Circle the correct answer.**

1 You ___ be right about her although I'm not absolutely sure.

a should   b must   (c) may

2 They ___ have too many meals at fast food restaurants.

a may not   b shouldn't   c ought to

3 I ___ listen to you, but just this once I will.

a ought not to   b should   c may

4 It ___ rain later – take an umbrella with you.

a should   b can't   c might

5 She ___ be your twin sister. She doesn't look at all like you!

a mustn't   b can't   c may not

6 You ___ to finish your homework before you go out.

a ought   b should   c must

7 We ___ go camping this summer, but I'd prefer to stay in a hotel.

a should to   b ought   c might

8 That ___ be the best piece of news I've heard for a long time!

a can't   b must   c should

7 **Complete the dialogue with the words from the box.**

| can't | may | ~~might~~ | must | ought | should |

Jasia: Mae ¹ _____ might _____ have a party on Saturday.

Carl: Yes, we ² _____ to buy her something. It ³ _____ be her birthday.

Sue: Yes, I think it is. We ⁴ _____ buy her some snow boots!

Jasia: Why? Is she going skiing?

Carl: That ⁵ _____ be right. The weather is not cold enough for snow!

Sue: Well, I heard on the news that it ⁶ _____ snow at the weekend!

Jasia: Well anyway, let's buy her something nice!

Think about it!

You can say that you *should* or *shouldn't* do something because it is either good for you or bad for you.

8 **Complete the text by writing one word in each gap. There may be more than one possible answer.**

Today is a bad day for the Westford family. Everyone is in a bad mood. Why? Well, Dad

¹ _____ might _____ have to find a new job because his firm doesn't need him anymore.

Mum ² _____ to go to the dentist's because she has had toothache for two days.

Phil ³ _____ do a lot of work on his computer, but it isn't working properly. Liz's best

friend has just gone to the USA for two years and ⁴ _____ not come back at all, so she

⁵ _____ be happy. What ⁶ _____ we do to make them feel better, I wonder?

9 **Look at the list below and tick (✔) the items you agree with. Then write sentences with** *should, shouldn't, ought to* **or** *ought not to.*

How to live healthily

watch a lot of TV
exercise every day
eat lots of fresh fruit and vegetables
eat lots of fried foods
drink a lot of fizzy drinks
drink a lot of water
go swimming regularly
play computer games for hours
eat sweets all day long
get plenty of sleep

1 You shouldn't watch a lot of TV because it's bad
for your eyes. _____
2 _____
3 _____
4 _____
5 _____
6 _____
7 _____
8 _____
9 _____
10 _____

10 **Find the mistakes in the sentences. Then write them correctly.**

1 The door is locked. Daniel <u>should</u> be out.

   The door is locked. Daniel must be out.

2 If you have toothache, you might go to the dentist's.

   _____

3 We might to come and see you on Sunday.

   _____

4 He can be the new boss. He's too young!

   _____

5 We ought water the plants or they will die.

   _____

6 You should to apologise to him.

   _____

Pairwork

Work in pairs. Take turns to talk about what job you may or may not do in the future and how you will train for it.

Writing

It is the summer holidays and you have had a letter from a friend who is bored and has nothing to do. He/She has asked you for some advice about what he/she should do in their spare time. Write back, giving him/her your ideas.

Dear _____ ,

Thank you for your letter. It was really good to hear from you.

Well, I've got some ideas about how you can spend your spare time.

Firstly, you could _____

_____

_____ .

Also, you ought to _____ .

It may be a good idea to _____ .

Write to me and let me know what you decide to do.

Best,

_____

Conditionals

First conditional

The first conditional is formed as follows:

If + present simple, future simple

*If she **studies**, she **will pass** the exam.*

We use the first conditional to talk about something that will probably happen.

*If I **see** Charlotte, **I'll tell** her your news.*

*If he **isn't** well tomorrow, he **won't go** to work.*

Notes

When we ask a question in the first conditional, the *if* clause does not change. The question form appears in the result clause.

*If you **see** her, **will** you **tell** her to phone me?*

*If you **get** there early, **will** you **phone** me?*

---

1 **Complete the sentences with the first conditional and the words in brackets.**

1 If she stops eating sweets, _____ she will be healthier _____ (be healthier).

2 If it rains, _____ (we / stay at home).

3 If I eat less sugar, _____ (lose weight).

4 If we get up early, _____ (go out for the day).

5 If he works in the summer, _____ (earn lots of money).

6 If you don't stop copying my work, _____ (I / tell the teacher).

7 If he doesn't get enough sleep, _____ (become ill).

8 If they learn the song, _____ (sing it to us).

2 **Complete the sentences with the first conditional.**

1 If you _____see_____ (see) Jana, will you give her a message?

2 If he _____ (arrive) early, he will be able to meet my parents.

3 If she _____ (not have) too much homework, she will come and see us.

4 The weather _____ (be) freezing tomorrow if it snows.

5 If you work with those paints, you _____ (get) dirty.

6 They won't visit us if you _____ (be) too busy.

7 Will you take the medicine if I _____ (buy) it for you?

8 I _____ (not go) swimming tomorrow if it is cold.

9 If the food isn't hot, he _____ (not eat) it.

10 You _____ (feel) tired tomorrow if you don't go to sleep now.

Unless

Unless can be used in first conditional sentences. It means *if not*.

Unless you ask your parents first, we won't take you to the concert.
(If you don't ask your parents first, we won't take you to the concert.)

Unless it rains, we'll go for a picnic tomorrow.
(If it doesn't rain, we'll go for a picnic tomorrow.)

---

3 **Complete the sentences with *unless* and the words from the box.**

apologise	clean his dirty boots	eat healthy food	hurry up
~~pay attention~~	save some money	train hard	water the plants

1 _____Unless you pay attention_____ , you won't understand the lesson.

2 _____ , he won't get into the team.

3 _____ , he will miss the plane.

4 _____ , I won't ever speak to you again!

5 _____ , I won't let him come into this house!

6 _____ , you won't lose any weight.

7 _____ , they will die.

8 _____ , we won't be able to buy a new computer.

Second conditional

The second conditional is formed as follows:

If + past simple, *would* + infinitive
*If they **wanted** to take part, they **would** tell us.*

We use the second conditional:

- to talk about something which is impossible.
  *If I **were** a millionaire, I **would** have my own jet aeroplane.*

- to talk about something that is possible but unlikely.
  *If they **asked** him, he **would** probably say no.*

- to give advice, usually with the phrase *If I were you, ...*
  *If I **were** you, I**'d** be more careful about your homework.*

4 **Complete the sentences with the second conditional.**

1 If we _____wanted_____ (want) more money, we ____would ask____ (ask) for it.

2 If he _____ (not do) his homework on time, the teacher _____ (be) disappointed.

3 If I _____ (be) you, I _____ (tell) him what you think.

4 She _____ (bake) us a cake if we _____ (ask) her nicely!

5 If you _____ (not have) such a lot of homework, I _____ (invite) you for a bike ride.

6 Your parents _____ (not worry) about you if you _____ (tell) them the truth.

7 If I _____ (not go) to the gym every week, I _____ (not be) very fit.

8 If it _____ (not be) so cold, I _____ (go) for a walk.

9 If the jeans _____ (be) cheaper, I _____ (buy) them.

10 They _____ (worry) if we _____ (not phone) them as soon as we arrived.

5 **Complete the sentences in your own words.**

1 I feel lonely.
   If I were you, _____I'd phone my friends_____ .

2 I get bad marks in my exams.
   If I were you, _____ .

3 I feel tired all the time.
   If I were you, _____ .

4 I feel stressed and worried.
   If I were you, _____ .

5 My friends don't understand me.
   If I were you, _____ .

6 I'm always bored.
   If I were you, _____ .

Third conditional

The third conditional is formed as follows:

If + past perfect, *would* + *have* + past participle

If I **had left** *the party earlier, I* **would have missed** *the best part of the evening.*

If I **hadn't stayed up** *late last night, I* **would have got up** *earlier this morning.*

We use the third conditional to talk about something in the past which was a possibility but didn't happen.

If you **had come** *with us, you* **would have had** *a nice time.*

If he **hadn't had** *an argument with his dad, he* **would have come** *to the party.*

6 **Complete the sentences with the third conditional.**

1 If I hadn't missed the bus, _____ I wouldn't have arrived late _____ (I / not arrive / late).

2 If they hadn't talked in class, _____ (teacher / not send / them out).

3 If I hadn't remembered in time, _____ (I / burn / the dinner).

4 The house would have burnt down _____ (I / not call / the fire brigade).

5 If you hadn't left the cage open, _____ (the parrot / not escape).

6 If you hadn't broken the window, _____ (Mum / not be / upset).

7 They wouldn't have won the prize _____ (they / not work / so hard).

8 Sarah wouldn't have been late _____ (she / not get / lost).

Think about it!

If the conditional sentence does not start with the *if* clause, we do not need a comma.

7 **Complete the sentences with the third conditional.**

1 If she _____ had tried _____ (try) harder, she _____ would have got _____ (get) better marks.

2 If Lana _____ (not be) late, she _____ (see) the beginning of the film.

3 If they _____ (eat) all the food, there _____ (not be) anything left for us!

4 If the cardboard boxes _____ (not be) so heavy, we _____ (move) them.

5 She _____ (buy) those shoes if her mother _____ (agree).

6 Our friends _____ (say) 'yes' if they _____ (want) to come with us.

7 The artist _____ (paint) your picture if you _____ (give) him more time.

8 If you _____ (wait) any longer, we _____ (miss) the train.

9 She _____ (not know) about the test if we _____ (not tell) her.

10 The flowers _____ (not die) if you _____ (water) them.

8 Find the extra word and write it in the space.

1 If you <u>have</u> had arrived earlier, you would have met my brother. _____have_____

2 She will do the shopping if she will has time. _____

3 If you were had done the work on time, you wouldn't have been in trouble. _____

4 Will you tell him the truth if he does asks you? _____

5 If you listened to her, you would to find her very interesting. _____

6 They wouldn't have bought the shirt if they had been known how expensive it was. _____

7 They'll build a new house unless if they have enough money. _____

8 If my friends have had more spare time, they would do more sport. _____

9 Circle the correct answer.

1 He wouldn't have *be* / (*been*) angry if she had told him the truth.

2 Unless the weather *improves* / *improve*, we won't go out tomorrow.

3 *If* / *Unless* she leaves now, she'll be in time to catch the last bus.

4 The lunch *will* / *won't* be ready by one o'clock if you don't start cooking now.

5 If they *wouldn't* / *hadn't* invited us to stay, we wouldn't have visited them.

6 If you *won* / *win* a lot of money, would you buy a house by the sea?

7 If your parents *would let* / *let* you, would you get a cat?

8 If the television *stopped* / *did stop* working, what would you do?

10 Rewrite the second sentence with a similar meaning to the first.

1 I haven't got much time, so I can't stay any longer.

If I had more time, I _____would stay longer_____ .

2 He wanted to buy a laptop, but it was too expensive.

If he had had more money, he _____ .

3 I'll go ice-skating tomorrow unless my sister can't come with me.

I'll go ice-skating tomorrow if _____ .

4 She'll make her parents happy if she passes her exams.

She'll make her parents happy unless _____ .

5 He hadn't called his friend because he had been busy.

He would have called his friend if _____ .

6 The doctor said that I should take a few days off school.

The doctor said, 'If I were you, _____ .

7 They didn't have any toast for breakfast because there wasn't any bread.

If there had been some bread, _____ .

8 The students aren't working very hard because they are tired.

If the students weren't tired, _____ .

11 **Read the different situations and write what you would do in each one.**

1   If it snowed hard overnight, what would you do?

     I wouldn't go to school.

2   If you saw someone robbing a bank, what would you do?

3   If your best friend told your secrets to someone else, what would you do?

4   If you wanted to get fit, what would you do?

5   If you wanted to get a high mark in a test, what would you do?

6   If you missed the last bus home in the evening, what would you do?

7   If you didn't get the job you wanted very much, what would you do?

8   If you didn't remember a friend's birthday, what would you do?

Pairwork

Work in pairs. Take turns to ask and answer questions about what you would do in different situations.

For example:

What would you do if you saw a huge spider or a cockroach?

How would you feel if you were on the top of a very high mountain?

What would you do if you saw a rat?

Writing

Write about what you would do in the situations below.

Give reasons for what you write.

If I saw a ghost …

If I could travel through time …

Passive voice

The passive voice is formed with the verb *to be* and the past participle of the main verb.

- present simple: *am/are/is* + past participle
  *A lot of paintings **are stolen** each year.*

- present continuous: *am/are/is* + *being* + past participle
  *The meal **is being prepared** at the moment.*

- past simple: *was/were* + past participle
  *Our flat **was built** ten years ago.*

- past continuous: *was/were* + *being* + past participle
  *The visitors **were being shown** around the school.*

- present perfect simple: *have/has* + *been* + past participle
  *The winners **have already been chosen**.*

- past perfect simple: *had* + *been* + past participle
  *He **had been hurt** in an accident and was in hospital.*

- future simple: *will* + *be* + past participle
  *The new school **will be built** just down the road from our house.*

- future perfect simple: *will* + *have* + *been* + past participle
  *The presents **will have been bought** by tonight.*

- modals (present): *must/can*, etc. + *be* + past participle
  *The projects **must be finished** by the end of next week.*

That's so cool! A VR headset! I love new technology.

Actually, virtual reality was invented in the 1960s!

We use the passive voice:

- to emphasise the action rather than the person who did it (the agent).
  *The new hospital **was opened** today.*

- when we don't know who did the action.
  *My bike **was stolen** yesterday.*

- when it is easy to understand who did the action.
  *The man **was arrested** last night.*

Notes

We don't use the passive voice in the present perfect continuous, the past perfect continuous or the future continuous.

1 **Complete the sentences with the passive voice in the present simple or present continuous.**

1 A new airport _____ is being built _____ (build) outside London.
2 All her letters _____ (write) on the computer.
3 His car _____ (wash) every week.
4 The chicken _____ (cook) at the moment.
5 That ice cream _____ (make) from natural ingredients.
6 The party plans _____ (arrange) by my parents.
7 The students _____ (teach) by a new teacher this year.
8 Spanish _____ (speak) in many countries of the world.

2 **Complete the sentences with the verbs from the box. Use the passive voice in the past simple or past continuous.**

| build   eat   interview   make   prepare   watch   wear   write |

1 A new airport _____ was built _____ outside London.
2 The announcement _____ on social media.
3 The dress _____ by a famous model.
4 The fish _____ by the cat.
5 This essay _____ by the best student last year.
6 The meal _____ while we were talking.
7 This comedy series _____ by a lot of people.
8 The star _____ by the reporter while they were driving in a limousine.

Passive voice: questions and negatives

The negative is formed by putting the word *not* after the auxiliary verb.
*The furniture **will not be sold** today.*

The question is formed by putting the auxiliary verb before the subject.
*The furniture **will be sold** tomorrow.*   →   ***Will** the furniture **be sold** tomorrow?*

3 **Write questions.**

1 The lambs were fed.

   Were the lambs fed?

2 The room was being painted.

   _____

3 A chocolate cake is being baked.

   _____

4 The lawn was being mown.

   _____

5 Two men were interviewed by the police.

   _____

6 The homework is assigned on Tuesdays.

   _____

7 All the meals are cooked by the chef.

   _____

8 The seeds are being planted.

   _____

4 **Complete the sentences with the passive voice in the past perfect simple.**

1 The rabbit _____had been given_____ (give) a bath and its fur was white and clean.

2 The robbers _____ (catch) before the police arrived.

3 The lights _____ (not switch) off before we left the house.

4 All their things _____ (pack) into boxes when I got there.

5 The cake _____ (not make), so I went back the next day.

6 The book _____ (write) before the film was made.

7 The coffee and toast _____ (make) before the guests sat down to breakfast.

8 They _____ (not invite) to such an expensive restaurant before.

5 **Complete the sentences with the passive voice. Use the modal verb in brackets and a verb from the box.**

| cancel   deliver   find   finish   give   need   test   touch |

1 This project _____must be finished_____ (must) by next week.

2 Your eyes _____ (should) every six months.

3 These extra chairs _____ (might) for the party.

4 The parcel _____ (could) tomorrow.

5 This electric wire _____ (mustn't) by anyone.

6 The match _____ (may) because of the bad weather.

7 Her books _____ (can) in all good bookshops.

8 These pills _____ (shouldn't) to children.

6 **Write sentences.**

1 not all the tickets / for the concert / sell / yet

Not all the tickets for the concert have been
sold yet.

2 the project / complete / next week

_____

_____

3 the results / of the exam / announce / tomorrow

_____

_____

4 the kitchen / paint / yellow / last year

_____

_____

5 the baby / be born / next week

_____

_____

6 lunch / not prepare / until later

_____

_____

Changing from active to passive

Tense	Active voice	Passive voice
Present simple	He finishes the work.	The work is finished.
Present continuous	He is finishing the work.	The work is being finished.
Past simple	He finished the work.	The work was finished.
Past continuous	He was finishing the work.	The work was being finished.
Present perfect simple	He has finished the work.	The work has been finished.
Past perfect simple	He had finished the work.	The work had been finished.
Future simple	He will finish the work.	The work will be finished.
Future perfect simple	He will have finished the work.	The work will have been finished.
modals (present)	He must finish the work.	The work must be finished.

We change a sentence from the active to the passive voice in the following way:
- The object of the active sentence becomes the subject of the passive sentence.
- We use the verb _to be_ in the same tense as the verb in the active sentence.
- We use the past participle of the main verb in the active sentence.
- We use the word _by_ if we want to say who did the action.

Mum made the chocolate cake. → _The chocolate cake **was made by** Mum._
They have eaten the biscuits. → _The biscuits **have been eaten**._

7 Change the sentences from active to passive voice.

1 The teacher is checking her homework.

Her homework is being checked by the teacher.

2 They took the visitors to the train station.

_____

3 They were preparing the students for the exam.

_____

4 He has asked his friends to come to the concert.

_____

5 Someone took their bags to their rooms.

_____

6 Someone will clean his room tomorrow.

_____

7 You mustn't leave the computer on.

_____

8 He always writes his emails in the morning.

_____

9 I can find the books in the library.

_____

10 You should answer your text messages from friends.

_____

Think about it!

We only include *by* … if it is absolutely necessary in order to understand the sentence.

---

8 Rewrite the sentences using the word in bold. Use between two and five words.

1 No one has seen his car for days. **been**

His car _____ hasn't been seen _____ for days.

2 They are repairing his bike at the moment. **being**

His bike _____ at the moment.

3 My uncle grows wheat on his farm. **is**

Wheat _____ on my uncle's farm.

4 The guide showed us around the castle. **by**

We were _____ the guide.

5 They had eaten all the cakes by the time we got there. **had**

All the cakes _____ by the time we got there.

6 Millions of people all over the world were watching the concert. **was**

The concert _____ millions of people all over the world.

9 **Complete the article with the passive voice in the correct form.**

Several areas of Italy [1] _____*were hit*_____ (hit) yesterday by bad storms. Many farms
[2] _____ (flood) and people [3] _____ (force) to go up
onto the roofs of their houses. They [4] _____ (rescue) by firefighters and
escaped to dry land. The weather [5] _____ (expect) to improve at the weekend.

Two men [6] _____ (arrest) last night for stealing a television and money from
a house. A police officer [7] _____ (call) when neighbours heard bangs and
crashes coming from the house next door. The two men [8] _____ (put) in prison
for the night and tomorrow they will go to court.

A school in Manchester [9] _____ (give) a special award for its commitment to
musical learning. The award [10] _____ (announce) this morning. The school
says that the money from the award [11] _____ (use) to buy musical instruments
for the school in the coming year.

On Wednesday morning, an SOS signal [12] _____ (receive) from a fishing boat
that was in difficulty. Fortunately, all the fishermen [13] _____ (bring) to shore by
a lifeboat and [14] _____ (take) to hospital suffering from shock and cold.

Pairwork

Work in pairs. Take turns to ask and answer questions using the passive voice. Talk about the things that would be done for you if you won a lot of money.

Writing

Write a short paragraph about one of the two processes below. Use the passive voice. You can draw pictures or use photos to illustrate your writing.

- choosing players for a school sports team
- making a cake or other food

1 **Complete the sentences with the correct form of *can* and the verbs from the box.**

come   ~~not find~~   not go   have   not hear   help   open   not speak   understand

1   I _____can't find_____ anything in this drawer because it's such a mess!
2   You _____ to the library now – it's closed.
3   _____ I _____ a glass of water, please?
4   _____ you _____ the window, please?
5   I _____ French, but I _____ it very well.
6   _____ you _____ to my party on Saturday?
7   She _____ what the teacher is saying. She speaks so quietly.
8   We _____ you if you like.

2 **Complete the sentences with the correct form of *be able to* and the words in brackets.**

1   I'm sorry, but I _____won't be able to come_____ (not come) to my piano lesson tomorrow.
2   The boy _____ (not swim) across the pool, so he had a few more lessons.
3   I _____ (come) camping with you next summer!
4   Dad _____ (not go) to work for several days because he was ill.
5   _____ (you / phone) him yet?
6   When I was young, I _____ (not reach) the top cupboards in the kitchen.
7   They _____ (not lend) us their laptop tomorrow because it is broken.
8   _____ (you / play) the guitar when you were seven?

3 **Circle the correct answer.**

1   *Am I able to /* Could I have a break for a minute?
2   The door was stuck, but finally I *was able to / could* open it and leave the room.
3   *Could you / Are you able to* bring me a glass of orange juice, please?
4   I hope I'll *can / be able to* visit you in London next year.
5   They *can't / weren't able to* help us with our problems, but at least they listened to us.
6   He *could / is able to* teach English now because he passed his exams last year.
7   At the age of five, he *was able to / can* speak two languages.
8   As soon as we got to the restaurant, we *can / could* hear our friends laughing and chatting.

4 **Complete the sentences with the correct form of *must, mustn't, have to* or *don't have to* and the verb in brackets.**

1 I _____ must remember _____ (remember) to take my book back to the library tomorrow.

2 At some schools, children _____ (wear) school uniforms; they can wear what they like.

3 You _____ (jump) off the bus when it's moving.

4 I _____ (go) to the station to meet him because he is going to take a taxi.

5 We _____ (practise) our English more so we can speak to the tourists in the summer.

6 We _____ (be) late for lunch because there are other guests here.

7 He _____ (do) so much housework every day – the house is clean anyway!

8 You _____ (leave) your books lying around on the floor!

5 **Circle the correct answer.**

1 They ___ be very tired after that long walk!

   a can't   (b) must   c should

2 I ___ go and see Julie this evening – do you want to come?

   a may   b can't   c can

3 We ___ to leave now because it's getting late.

   a ought   b should   c must

4 That ___ right! I make the answer 500€.

   a can be   b mustn't be   c can't be

5 It ___ rain later, but you never know with English weather!

   a should   b must   c could

6 They ___ spend so much money on silly things.

   a may not   b shouldn't   c ought to

7 I ___ eat any more, but the food is so delicious!

   a ought not to   b should   c may

8 That ___ be the reason for their strange behaviour – perhaps we should ask them what is wrong.

   a mustn't   b can   c can't

6 **Complete the sentences with the first conditional.**

1 They _____ won't go _____ (not go) on the trip if Kenji _____ is _____ (be) still ill.

2 _____ (you / help) me if I _____ (show) you what to do?

3 I _____ (not go) to the park tomorrow if you _____ (not come) with me.

4 If the fish _____ (not be) fresh, he _____ (not eat) it.

5 If I _____ (concentrate), I know I _____ (do) well in the test.

6 You _____ (not manage) to get up early in the morning if you _____ (stay) up late.

7 If you _____ (see) Liza, _____ (you / tell) her that I'm expecting her tomorrow?

8 I _____ (be) late for school if I _____ (not catch) that bus.

7 **Write sentences using the second conditional.**

1   I / not practise tennis / every day / I / not get / into / the team

    If I didn't practise tennis every day, I wouldn't

    get into the team.

2   it / not be / so late at night / I / study / some more

    _____

    _____

3   these shoes / be / my size / I / buy / them

    _____

    _____

4   we / have / more time / we / have / more hobbies

    _____

    _____

5   I / be / very happy / you / come / to my birthday party

    _____

    _____

6   she / buy / new jeans / she / have / more money / ?

    _____

    _____

7   they / not drive / me to school / I / miss my first class

    _____

    _____

8   you / lend / me your bike / I / promise / to bring it back soon / ?

    _____

    _____

8 **Complete the sentences with the third conditional.**

1   If my friends had asked me to go, I _____ *would have refused* _____ (refuse).

2   If he had listened to the news, he _____ (heard) about the accident.

3   Sandor wouldn't have met her if he _____ (not go) to the party.

4   If I hadn't slept so late, we _____ (not miss) school.

5   If I hadn't been so tired, I _____ (not make) so many mistakes.

6   If there hadn't been a fire alarm, they _____ (not leave) the class.

7   Alan would have been happy if he _____ (pass) the exam.

8   The clothes would have dried out if it _____ (not rain) again.

9 **Write sentences with *unless*.**

1   We won't go out at the weekend if the weather is bad.

    We'll go out at the weekend unless the weather is bad.

2   You won't know what to do if you don't listen.

    _____

    _____

3   If you don't buy me some apples, I won't be able to make an apple pie.

    _____

    _____

4   You'll never finish your homework if you don't stop watching TV!

    _____

    _____

5   If he doesn't train hard, he won't be ready for the race.

    _____

    _____

6   If Mum doesn't get back late, we'll go to the cinema.

    _____

    _____

7   If her plans don't change, she'll leave for Australia in the summer.

    _____

    _____

8   If my friend doesn't like the idea, she won't join in the activity.

    _____

    _____

10 **Complete the sentences with the passive voice. Use the correct form.**

1 The cakes ___were baked___ (bake) by Granny.

2 The members of the tennis team _____ (choose) yesterday.

3 _____ this house _____ (build) by your great-grandfather?

4 The children _____ (take) to school by bus every day.

5 _____ these products _____ (make) here in the village?

6 A lot of oranges _____ (grow) in Spain.

7 My bedroom _____ (paint) last week.

8 The tests _____ (mark) by the teacher right now.

11 **Change the sentences from active to passive voice.**

1 We must pick the fruit as soon as it is ready.

The fruit must be picked as soon as it is ready.

2 People can visit the museum every day.

_____

_____

3 You shouldn't send food by post.

_____

_____

4 They had ordered a large pizza.

_____

_____

5 They will repair your computer tomorrow.

_____

_____

6 You mustn't leave the lights on all night.

_____

_____

7 By seven o'clock, they had put up the tent.

_____

_____

8 While we were talking, they were preparing the meal.

_____

_____

12 **Rewrite the sentences using the word in bold. Use between two and five words.**

1 They had eaten all the food by the time we arrived. **been**

All the food _____had been eaten_____ by the time we arrived.

2 They celebrated her birthday with a big party. **was**

Her birthday _____ with a big party.

3 Someone broke into the school last night. **was**

The school _____ last night.

4 They are repairing his bike at the moment. **being**

His bike _____ at the moment.

5 The teacher gave us all the information. **by**

We were _____ the teacher.

6 My uncle grows potatoes and tomatoes on his farm. **are**

Potatoes and tomatoes _____ on my uncle's farm.

7 I should return the library book by next week. **be**

The library book _____ by next week.

8 We might finish our project in time to go out. **be**

Our project _____ in time to go out.

I wish I had a sports car!

If only I had studied for that test.

Wish/if only + past simple

We use *wish/if only* + past simple when a situation is different from what we would like.

(I don't have a car.)
*I **wish**/**If only** I had a car.*
(I don't go out very often.)
*I **wish**/**If only** I went out more often.*

When we use the verb *to be*, we always use *were*.
***If only** I were rich.*
*He **wishes** he weren't so late.*

We often follow *wish/if only* with *could*.
*She **wishes** she could swim.*
***If only** I could speak Italian.*

Notes

Wish and *if only* have the same meaning. *If only* emphasises our desire for a different situation and is not used in the question form.

1 **Complete the sentences with the past simple.**

1 She wishes she _____didn't live_____ (live) in France.

2 He wishes he _____ (own) a new bike.

3 If only they _____ (can) go to the beach.

4 I wish I _____ (be) a famous film star.

5 If only he _____ (write) more neatly.

6 She wishes she _____ (know) more people.

7 Lots of people wish they _____ (not wear) glasses.

8 Do you wish you _____ (not have) a test this week?

> *Wish/if only* + past continuous
>
> We use *wish/if only* with the past continuous when we would like to be doing something different from what we are doing.
> *I **wish** I **was lying** on the beach.*
> *If only it **wasn't raining**.*

2 **Complete the sentences with the verbs from the box. Use the past continuous or past simple.**

> ~~eat~~   have   lie   listen   play   read   speak   not work

1 If only we ___were eating___ ice cream instead of chicken and potatoes!

2 Don't you wish you _____ on the beach at the moment?

3 I think those students wish they _____ to music.

4 I wish I _____ Spanish. It's a beautiful language.

5 She wishes she _____ on her project on such a lovely day.

6 My dad wishes he _____ football right now and not working in his office.

7 We wish we _____ new laptops instead of old computers.

8 If only I _____ my favourite magazine and not this one!

3 **Write sentences.**

1 My brother is a student. (rock star)

  My brother wishes he was a rock star.

2 Milo is short. (tall)

  _____

3 The children are sleeping on the floor. (sleep / in their beds)

  _____

4 I am bad at history. (good)

  _____

5 The football team is playing badly today. (play / well)

  _____

6 My mother has brown eyes. (blue)

  _____

7 Misha is walking to school. (drive / his dad's car)

  _____

8 Lara doesn't have many friends. (have / lots of friends)

  _____

Wish/if only + past perfect

We use *wish/if only* + past perfect to say that we are sorry about a past situation. It shows that we would like the situation to have been different.
(I didn't say good luck to my sister before her exam.)
I wish/If only I had said good luck to my sister before her exam.
(He was rude to his friend's mother.) *He wishes/If only he hadn't been rude to his friend's mother.*

4 Complete the sentences with the past perfect.

1 I wish I ___had listened___ (listen) to what the teacher said.

2 I wish I _____ (buy) some new clothes for the party.

3 He wishes he _____ (learn) how to fix his computer.

4 They wish they _____ (not agree) to study together on Saturday.

5 If only we _____ (not say) those rude things to him.

6 Do you wish you _____ (study) harder for that test?

7 If only I _____ (go) to the library that day.

8 Mum wishes we _____ (do) the housework for her.

5 Tick (✔) the correct sentence, *a* or *b*.

1 a I wish it had been sunny yesterday. ✔

  b I wish it have been sunny yesterday. ___

2 a Dad wishes he hadn't spent so much money on a new laptop. ___

  b Dad wishes he hasn't spent so much money on a new laptop. ___

3 a Do you wish you had gone to bed earlier last night? ___

  b Do you wish you had went to bed earlier last night? ___

4 a She wishes she had wrote a better essay. ___

  b She wishes she had written a better essay. ___

5 a If only I wish I had a longer holiday! ___

  b If only I had a longer holiday! ___

6 a They wish they had visit London Zoo when they were in England. ___

  b They wish they had visited London Zoo when they were in England. ___

7 a If only she hadn't forgotten her mother's birthday. ___

  b If only she hasn't forgotten her mother's birthday. ___

8 a They wish it wasn't raining. ___

  b They wish it hadn't raining. ___

6 **Match 1–8 with a–h.**

1 They wish they had brought
2 Do you wish you had cut
3 She wishes she had joined
4 They wish they hadn't eaten
5 If only the bus hadn't arrived
6 Jan wishes he hadn't ridden
7 We wish we had won
8 If only they had been

a the tennis club instead of the gym.
b more money in the lottery.
c late; we wouldn't have missed the start of the concert.
d their phones with them.
e so many sweets.
f more careful with their homework.
g your hair a different style?
h his bike into that street.

Wish/if only + would

We use *wish/if only* + *would* + infinitive:

- to say that we would like something to be different in the future.
  *They **wish** their parents **would** let them stay out late.*
  *He **wishes** she **wouldn't** ask so many questions!*

- to talk about something someone else does that annoys us.
  *I **wish** you **would** stop playing loud music!*
  *She **wishes** her husband **wouldn't** eat so much food!*

Notes

We use *wish/if only* + *would* + infinitive for actions, not states. We cannot use it when we are talking about our own behaviour.

7 **Write two sentences with *wish*.**

1 I / my piano teacher / criticise / me (praise)

  I wish my piano teacher wouldn't criticise me. I wish she would praise me.

2 I / my brother / shout at / me (talk to)

  _____

  _____

3 I / our cat / catch / mice (ignore)

  _____

  _____

4 I / you run / in the house (walk)

  _____

  _____

5 I / he close / the windows (open)

  _____

  _____

8 **Circle the correct answer.**

1 He wishes his dad would *to lend* / (*lend*) him his computer.

2 I wish you *won't* / *wouldn't* fight with your brother!

3 If only he would *is* / *be* more polite to his parents.

4 The students wish the English teacher *wasn't* / *wouldn't* test their grammar.

5 I wish my friend wouldn't *play* / *played* tricks on me all the time!

6 I wish you *would* / *will* come to see me next week.

7 Mum wishes I would *wear* / *to wear* smarter clothes.

8 I wish you *had* / *would* come on the cruise with us next summer.

Think about it!

We can use *could* instead of *would* to talk about desires for future possibilities.

---

9 **Rewrite the sentences using the word in bold. Use between two and five words.**

1 My brother bites his nails and I don't want him to. **wouldn't**

   I wish ____my brother wouldn't____ bite his nails.

2 It's raining and I want to go to the park. **was**

   I wish it _____ – then I could go to the park.

3 We haven't got a cat, but I want one. **wish**

   I _____ a cat.

4 I wanted to pass the English exam, but I didn't. **passed**

   I _____ the English exam.

5 She wants to be tall, but she isn't. **were**

   She _____ tall.

6 I really hope Mum buys me a new pair of trainers soon. **would**

   I wish _____ a new pair of trainers soon.

10 **Find the extra word and write it in the space.**

1 Do you wish you were <u>being</u> taller?

   _____being_____

2 They wish they had were living in another house. _____

3 She wishes she would had saved her money to buy a new computer.

   _____

4 If only the sun it would shine.

   _____

5 She wishes she had did seen her sister win the race. _____

6 Do you wish it would be snow?

   _____

7 My mum wishes I weren't been so lazy. _____

8 I wish if I were in the park instead of doing grammar exercises!

   _____

11 **Find the mistakes in the sentences. Then write them correctly.**

1   What do you wish you were <u>do</u> now?
    <u>What do you wish you were doing now?</u>

2   I wish you did help me with my homework.
    _____

3   Dana wishes she had taller.
    _____

4   Do you wish you would at the beach?
    _____

5   They wish they could had go to the party.
    _____

6   If only I hadn't would lost my purse.
    _____

12 **Complete the text by writing one word in each gap.**

My friends and I wish ¹ _____we_____ had worked harder for our exams. We ² _____
we had listened more in class. My best friend ³ _____ she had studied more maths and
some of my other friends wish they ⁴ _____ taken computer science as a subject. We all
⁵ _____ we had got better marks and that we ⁶ _____ have to take our exams
again! I wish I ⁷ _____ gone to the library and got the books I needed. Sometimes I wish
time ⁸ _____ go backwards – then I could do my revision again and work harder! But my
mother says it's never too late!

Pairwork

Work in pairs. Take turns to talk about things you wish you could change. Think about:

*   things you would change about your life today if you could.
*   things you wish you had or hadn't done in the past.
*   things you wish your parents would do.

Writing

Imagine you are a reporter and you have interviewed a prisoner. He has stolen money from people, he has stolen cars and he has robbed a bank. Now he is sorry for what he has done. Write your article, telling the readers what Jake wishes he had and hadn't done in the past.

Last week, I interviewed a man called Jake. Jake is in prison because he is a thief.

But Jake is sorry for what he's done. He wishes …

Reported speech: statements

Direct speech	Reported speech
Present simple	Past simple
'I live in Madrid,' he said.	He said he lived in Madrid.
Present continuous	Past continuous
'I am reading a book,' she said.	She said she was reading a book.
Past simple	Past perfect simple
'I wrote three emails,' said John.	John said he had written three emails.
Past continuous	Past perfect continuous
'I was living in London,' he said.	He said he had been living in London.
Present perfect simple	Past perfect simple
'I have lived in France,' said Ann.	Ann said she had lived in France.
Present perfect continuous	Past perfect continuous
'I've been working for hours,' she said.	She said she had been working for hours
will	would
'I will move to the country,' he said.	He said he would move to the country.
can	could
'I can play the guitar,' said Tim.	Tim said he could play the guitar.
must	had to
'I must go,' he said.	He said he had to go.

I spoke to your teacher yesterday.

What did she say?

She said she wanted you to do your homework more often!

We use reported speech when we tell someone what another person said.
'I am tired,' he said.
*He **said** he **was** tired.*

The tenses change as in the examples in the table on the previous page.
'I saw her at the bank,' he said.
*He **said** he **had seen** her at the bank.*

We also change personal pronouns, possessive adjectives and possessive pronouns.
'I want to borrow your book,' Henry told Sarah.
*Henry told Sarah **he wanted** to borrow **her** book.*

Notes

We can use the word *that* after *he/she said.*
He said he had to feed the dog.
*He said **that** he had to feed the dog.*

1 **Rewrite the sentences in reported speech.**

1 'I'm on the tennis team,' said Lev.

   Lev said he was on the tennis team.

2 'We are good students,' said Tori and Chris.

   _____

3 'I'm going to school,' said Eva.

   _____

4 'I've been waiting for ages,' said Alex.

   _____

5 'I can write excellent essays!' said Nick.

   _____

6 'I must buy a new pair of jeans,' said Mantoj.

   _____

7 'I'll see you tomorrow,' said Shura.

   _____

8 'We arrived late,' said the guests.

   _____

2 **Rewrite the dialogue in reported speech.**

1 **Paola:** 'I'm going to the shop.'

   Paola said she was going to the shop.

2 **Fabio:** 'I want to go too because I want some biscuits.'

   _____

3 **Paola:** 'I'll wait for you to get ready.'

   _____

4 **Fabio:** 'We can go to the shoe shop too because I need some trainers.'

   _____

5 **Paola:** 'That's a good idea. I'm going to the bookshop too.'

   _____

6 **Fabio:** 'I'll get my wallet and then we can go.'

   _____

3 Complete the sentences.

1 Sue said she had visited lots of countries.

'I _____have been to_____ lots of countries,' said Sue.

2 Leo and Otis said they were working hard.

'We _____ hard,' said Leo and Otis.

3 Dad said he was very tired.

'I _____ tired,' said Dad.

4 Eloisa said she was making cheese sandwiches for lunch.

'I _____ cheese sandwiches for lunch,' said Eloisa.

5 Karla said she would definitely come to the party.

'I _____ to the party,' said Karla.

6 Maria said she had been reading a magazine.

I _____ a magazine,' said Maria.

7 Zach said he could repair the computer.

'I _____ the computer,' said Zach.

8 Eduardo said he could help me with my project.

'I _____ with your project,' said Eduardo.

4 Circle the correct answer.

1 She said she ___ understand English television programmes.

   a   can   b   was   c   could

2 The girls said that they ___ never eaten grapefruit!

   a   had   b   have   c   did

3 Ceci said she ___ meet us outside the museum.

   a   will   b   can   c   would

4 My mother said she ___ make all the food for the party.

   a   can   b   could   c   has

5 Kasper said he sometimes ___ study at the weekends.

   a   must   b   have to   c   had to

6 They said they ___ learning to snowboard.

   a   are   b   were   c   have

7 Delja said she ___ very tired.

   a   is   b   has been   c   was

8 The teacher said Raj ___ good progress.

   a   was making   b   made   c   makes

Say and *tell*

Say and *tell* are the two introductory verbs we usually use with reported speech.

We use the verb *tell* with an object.
*He **told us** she wasn't feeling very well.*
*I **told my mother** I would be late.*

We use the verb *say* without an object.
*He **said** she wasn't feeling very well.*
*I **said** I would be late.*

5 **Complete the sentences with *said* or *told*.**

1   I _____told_____ the teacher I hadn't done all my homework.

2   He _____ he was going to the gym to do some exercise.

3   The teacher _____ us she had marked our essays.

4   Cindy _____ she had seen him.

5   The computer technician _____ me she couldn't repair my laptop.

6   Martin _____ he had read everything William Shakespeare ever wrote.

7   Maribel _____ her friends that she was having a party.

8   The police officer _____ the thief that he was under arrest.

Changes in time and place

There are also other changes that take place when we use reported speech.

today	→	*that day*
tonight	→	*that night*
tomorrow	→	*the following day/the next day*
yesterday	→	*the day before/the previous day*
last year	→	*the year before/the previous year*
next week	→	*the week after/the following week*
a month ago	→	*a month before/the previous month*
now	→	*then*
at the moment	→	*at that moment*
here	→	*there*
this/these	→	*that/those*

'I saw a tiger at the zoo yesterday,' said Megan.
Megan said she had seen a tiger at the zoo **the day before**.

'I left my keys here,' said Hakim.
Hakim said he had left his keys **there**.

6 **Rewrite the sentences in reported speech.**

1 'I can meet you later,' said Sami.

   Sami said he could meet me later.

2 'I'll see you all tomorrow,' said the teacher.

   _____

3 'I saw this film two weeks ago,' said Aurek.

   _____

4 'She will be here at eight o'clock,' said David.

   _____

5 'We're going on holiday next week,' said Jo and Tim.

   _____

6 'I'm eating my breakfast now,' said Winek.

   _____

7 'I saw Leo yesterday,' said my aunt.

   _____

8 'It is my birthday today,' said Claudia.

   _____

Think about it!

Do not forget to change tenses, pronouns and time and place words!

7 **Circle the correct answer.**

1 Charlotte said she might take guitar lessons the (following) / next year.
2 My brother said he had wanted to stay in bed all day *the previous* / *before* day.
3 They said they were not eating sweets the *next* / *following* month.
4 I told Xavier I had lost my purse the day *previous* / *before*.
5 She said she didn't want anything to eat *then* / *now*.
6 The teacher told the students to read *this* / *that* book.
7 Jane said she was happy to be *there* / *here* when she arrived.
8 Cassian and Jim said they were joining the gym the *previous* / *following* year.

8 Complete the sentences.

1 Daniel said he liked the film he had seen the previous day.

'I _____liked the film I saw yesterday_____ ,' said Daniel.

2 Natasha said she wanted to visit her cousins the following year.

'I _____ ,' said Natasha.

3 Stuart said he had heard the news the day before.

'I _____ ,' said Stuart.

4 Lucia said she could help me then.

'I _____ ,' said Lucia.

5 Silas said he had to buy a new notebook the following week.

'I _____ ,' said Silas.

6 Aroon and Leah said they were going skateboarding that day.

'We _____ ,' said Aroon and Lee.

9 Complete the sentences with the words from the box.

| been (x2)   could   couldn't   had   have   was   will   would (x2) |

1 Anna said she _____would_____ be learning Spanish the following year.

2 I told my teacher I _____ understand what she had said.

3 My friend said she had _____ at the library.

4 They said they _____ meet me later that afternoon.

5 He said he didn't know where I _____ .

6 I _____ come to the park with you,' said Adeline.

7 Sharon said she had _____ waiting for me for ages.

8 Dad said he _____ worked late that evening.

9 'We _____ been studying for hours,' said Takeshi and Steven.

10 Peng said she _____ help me do the project.

10 **Find the mistakes in the sentences. Then write them correctly.**

1   'I bought your present <u>the previous day</u>,' said Michelle.

    <u>'I bought your present yesterday,' said Michelle.</u>

2   Amrit said he had forgot to lock the house the previous day.

     _____

3   Adam said he is driving to work the following day.

     _____

4   They all said the party the day previous had been great.

     _____

5   Marina said she has liked my new hairstyle.

     _____

6   Brian said he had to stay in tonight.

     _____

11 **Complete the text by writing one word in each gap.**

I was talking to my friend on the phone yesterday. He [1] _____ told _____ me that he
had been on holiday to Italy the [2] _____ week. He [3] _____ Italy
was a very interesting place to visit. He and his family [4] _____ walked all
round St Mark's Square and they had thrown some money into the fountain. They had
also seen the Leaning Tower of Pisa. He said it [5] _____ an unusual building
and that it [6] _____ been smaller than he had expected. We talked about
our school work and he [7] _____ me that he had [8] _____ getting
good marks in English. He said his mum was very pleased about that and she had said
she [9] _____ buy him a new bike if he continued to do well. Before he hung
up, he said he [10] _____ coming to visit me for the weekend. We agreed we
would go for a pizza in town – that might remind him of his holiday in Italy!

12 **Answer the questions in your own words.**

1   What has your teacher told you about in this lesson?

My teacher has told me about reported speech.

2   What did you say to your best friend yesterday?

3   What has the person sitting next to you in your English lesson said to you today?

4   What did the last person you spoke to at school yesterday say to you?

5   What did your mother/father say to you before you left the house?

6   What have you said to your teacher in this lesson?

Pairwork

Work in pairs. Take turns to talk about things that your parents, brothers, sisters or friends have said to you in the past week.

Writing

Imagine that you have just had a long conversation with your cousin in the USA. Now the rest of your family want to know what news your cousin had. Tell your family what your cousin said using reported speech.

Reported speech: *Wh-* questions

Direct speech	Reported speech
Present simple	Past simple
'Where are you?' she asked.	*She asked where I was.*
Present continuous	Past continuous
'Why are you crying?' he asked.	*He asked why I was crying.*
Past simple	Past perfect simple
'Who knocked on the door?' asked Kay.	*Kay asked who had knocked on the door.*
Past continuous	Past perfect continuous
'What was he doing?' she asked.	*She asked what he had been doing.*
Present perfect simple	Past perfect simple
'Where have they been?' he asked.	*He asked where they had been.*
Present perfect continuous	Past perfect continuous
'How long have you been living here?' she asked.	*She asked how long I had been living there.*
will	would
'When will you tell me?' asked Jim.	*Jim asked when I would tell him.*
can	could
'Which boy can speak English?' he asked.	*He asked which boy could speak English.*
must	had to
'Where must you go now?' she asked.	*She asked me where I had to go then.*

Who was that?

It was my Dad.
He asked where I was!

In reported speech, questions are introduced by the verb *ask*.
*She **asked** what time it was.*

We use the same question word that is in the direct question.
'Why did she come?' he asked.
*He **asked** why she had come.*

The verb comes after the subject, as in ordinary statements.
*He **asked** when we were going to tidy our bedrooms.*

Notes

The changes in time and place that you learnt in Unit 14 apply to reported questions.

1 Complete the sentences with *said* or *asked*.

1   They _____said_____ that they were going on holiday the following day.
2   He _____ what I was wearing to the party.
3   My mum _____ the teacher why I hadn't got good marks in English.
4   The teacher _____ that I hadn't studied hard enough.
5   The police officer _____ me where I had been the previous evening.
6   He _____ he had bought a present for his friend.
7   She _____ him what the present was.
8   I _____ my friend how long she was going to be away for.

2 Complete the sentences with the words from the box.

how   what (x2)   where   which   who   why (x2)

1   The passengers asked the crew _____what_____ time they were going to land.
2   The bus driver asked the boy _____ he was going.
3   The teacher asked me _____ classroom I was going to.
4   The doctor asked me _____ I was feeling.
5   The waiter asked us _____ we wanted to eat.
6   She asked him _____ he was laughing.
7   I asked my friend _____ she stopped playing tennis.
8   The taxi driver asked his passenger _____ he was going to meet.

3 **Complete the sentences.**

1 'What are you buying in town tomorrow?' she asked. She asked what _____I was buying_____ in town the following day.

2 'Which is your favourite book?' he asked. He asked which _____ .

3 'Why are you waiting here?' she asked. She asked why _____ there.

4 'Where do you live?' Taylor asked. Taylor asked _____ .

5 'Who are you meeting this evening?' John asked. John asked _____ that evening.

6 'When will the lesson be over?' we asked. We asked _____ over.

7 'How are you getting to school today?' Andrew asked. Andrew asked _____ that day.

8 'Why are you leaving so early?' Sheryl asked. Sheryl asked _____ so early.

9 'Where are the books?' David asked. David asked _____ .

10 'Who have you invited to the party?' she asked. She asked _____ to the party.

4 **Rewrite the sentences in direct speech.**

1 The teacher asked what we wanted her to explain.
 'What do you want me to explain?'

2 She asked who had broken the vase.
 _____

3 He asked the coach when the next match was going to take place.
 _____

4 We asked where they were going.
 _____

5 Mum asked me who I was meeting in town.
 _____

6 He asked why she didn't want to see him again.
 _____

7 Jarek asked what time I would arrive.
 _____

8 The teacher asked why I hadn't done my homework.
 _____

Reported speech: questions

Direct speech	Reported speech
Present simple	Past simple
'Are you tired?' she asked.	She asked if/whether I was tired.
Present continuous	Past continuous
'Is he watching television?' they asked.	They asked if/whether he was watching television.
Past simple	Past perfect simple
'Did Mark give you the money?' he asked.	He asked if/whether Mark had given me the money.
Past continuous	Past perfect continuous
'Were the children playing?' asked Sue.	Sue asked if/whether the children had been playing.
Present perfect simple	Past perfect simple
'Have you finished the book?' he asked.	He asked if/whether I had finished the book.
Present perfect continuous	Past perfect continuous
'Has he been working all day?' asked David.	David asked if/whether he had been working all day.
will	would
'Will you help me?' she asked.	She asked if/whether I would help her.
can	could
'Can he come out to play?' they asked.	They asked if/whether he could come out to play
must	had to
'Must we leave so early?' I asked.	I asked if/whether we had to leave so early.

When a direct question does not begin with a question word, we make the reported question with the word *if* or *whether*. The changes in tense and word order are the same.
*He asked **if** she had arrived.*
*He asked **whether** she had arrived.*

5 **Rewrite the sentences with *if/whether* in the correct place.**

1   He asked me I could help him to do his homework.

　He asked me if I could help him to do his homework.

2   They asked us we were going to play basketball.

_____

3   Mum asked me I wanted to watch TV that evening.

_____

4   I asked him it was cold outside.

_____

5   The teacher asked us we could write an essay about the environment.

_____

6   The commentator asked the spectators they were enjoying the race.

_____

6 **Rewrite the questions in reported speech.**

1 'Do you know how to use this computer?' Ken asked me.

   Ken asked me if I knew how to use that computer.

2 'Have you been waiting long?' she asked me.

   _____

3 'Can I borrow your pen?' Amida asked her friend.

   _____

4 'Was it raining this morning?' I asked.

   _____

5 'Am I doing well?' I asked the gym instructor.

   _____

6 'Have you ever been to Scotland?' we asked our teacher.

   _____

7 'Is it time to go home?' she asked.

   _____

8 'Are you in pain?' the nurse asked the patient.

   _____

9 'Did you go to the cinema last night?' Kelly asked me.

   _____

10 'Will you drive me into town?' Angie asked her dad.

   _____

Reported speech: commands and requests

Reported commands are usually introduced with the verb *tell* + object + infinitive with *to*.
Mum **told me to be** quiet.

If the command is negative, we put the word *not* before *to*.
'Don't open the window,' she said.
She **told me not to open** the window.

Reported requests are usually introduced with the verb *ask* + object + infinitive with *to*.
They **asked us to check in** on time.

If the request is negative, we put the word *not* before *to*.
'Don't be late,' she said.
She **asked them not to be** late.

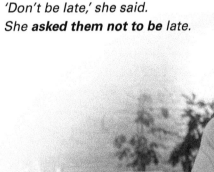

7 **Complete the sentences with *told* or *said*.**

1 The ticket collector _____said_____ he wanted to see our train tickets.

2 The ticket collector _____ us to show him our tickets.

3 He _____ his dad not to be disappointed with his exam results.

4 They _____ it was a boring film.

5 Dad _____ me to have my hair cut.

6 The police officer _____ the thief not to move.

7 The teacher _____ we shouldn't worry about the test.

8 She _____ her brother to sit down.

8 **Rewrite the sentences with *to* in the correct place.**

1 They asked us help them with their English homework.

They asked us to help them with their English
homework.

2 Dad told our neighbours not make so much noise late at night.

_____

_____

3 The secretary asked the visitors wait in the reception.

_____

_____

4 The swimming instructor told us concentrate on our breathing.

_____

_____

5 The teacher told the students not copy each other's work.

_____

_____

6 I asked my grandfather tell me about his life when he was young.

_____

_____

7 I told my friend stop shouting!

_____

_____

8 She told them do their homework.

_____

_____

9 **Rewrite the commands and requests in reported speech.**

1 'Open the window, please,' said Danny.

Danny asked me to open the window.

2 'Stop playing football in your bedroom!' Dad said to us.

_____

_____

3 'Don't be late home tonight!' Mum said to me.

_____

_____

4 'Be home by eleven o'clock!' Dad said to Dominik.

_____

_____

5 'Tidy your room!' Mum said to Sarah.

_____

_____

6 'Please phone me back,' my best friend said to me.

_____

_____

Think about it!

We do not use the word *please* when we change direct requests into reported requests.

10 **Rewrite the sentences in direct speech.**

1 Dad told me not to be so rude.

   'Don't be so rude!'

2 The neighbour told the boys to stop throwing stones.

   _____

   _____

3 I asked my sister to wake me up at seven o'clock.

   _____

   _____

4 My brother asked me to lend him some money.

   _____

   _____

5 My friend told me to hurry up.

   _____

   _____

6 The teacher told us to sit down and wait quietly for her to come back.

   _____

   _____

7 The guard told us not to take photographs of the paintings.

   _____

   _____

8 The students asked the teacher to give them more time to revise.

   _____

   _____

11 **Tick (✔) the correct sentence, *a* or *b*.**

1 a He told me to not be so noisy. ___
  b He told me not to be so noisy. ✔

2 a I told Mum that I am going to buy some new shoes. ___
  b I told Mum that I was going to buy some new shoes. ___

3 a They asked why I was waiting for the bus. ___
  b They said why I was waiting for the bus. ___

4 a I told my best friend to be careful when she went to London. ___
  b I told my best friend be careful when you go to London. ___

5 a The conductor asked the violinists to play more loudly. ___
  b The conductor asked the violinists that they play more loudly. ___

6 a Dad asked why had the package arrived late that morning. ___
  b Dad asked why the package had arrived late that morning. ___

7 a The woman said the man to get out of his car. ___
  b The woman told the man to get out of his car. ___

8 a Mum asked me make the lunch that day. ___
  b Mum asked me to make the lunch that day. ___

12 **Find the extra word and write it in the space.**

1 The shop assistant told the customer if she couldn't have a refund. _____if_____

2 I asked Joanna do not to bring her new friend to my house. _____

3 He asked her please to buy him some bread. _____

4 Frank said he told hadn't been waiting long when I arrived. _____

5 I asked whether Lizzie if she had ever visited London. _____

6 Granny asked me to have visit her the next time I was in the area. _____

7 The basketball trainer asked me whether or not if I had played before. _____

8 I asked Emily whether how long she was going to be in the library. _____

13 **Complete the text by writing one word in each gap.**

My friend and I went to stay in a hotel in London last month. When we arrived,

the man at the door [1]_____asked_____ us if we had already booked a room. We

[2]_____ him that we had and then he asked us [3]_____ go to the

reception desk. The receptionist [4]_____ us to show her our passports, and

then she [5]_____ us we had to fill in a form with our names and addresses.

She told us we [6]_____ staying in room 216 and she said someone

[7]_____ carry our bags upstairs for us. The man who helped us with our

bags was very nice – he told us that there [8]_____ lots of interesting sights

to see in London and he said we [9]_____ buy a tourist map at the reception

desk of the hotel if we wanted one. My friend said she [10]_____ tired and

that she was going to have a shower and lie down. But I told her [11]_____

to be so lazy – I said we [12]_____ to go straight out and start sightseeing!

She asked me why I was in such a hurry – but she agreed to come with me in the end.

We saw all the sights and we had a great time in London!

Pairwork

Work in pairs. Take turns to ask questions and report them using reported speech.

For example:

'Where do you live?' → She/He asked where I lived.

Writing

Choose one of the situations from the list below and write a report about what the people said to you, asked you or told you and what your replies were. Use reported speech.

• joining a club to learn something new

• going online to buy something

• going to parties to meet new friends

Adjectives and adverbs

> Did you see the film with Angelo Farrera?

> No, who's he?

> He's that handsome, tall, dark, Spanish actor.

> Now I want to see it!

Adjective order

When there are a number of adjectives in a phrase, we put them in the following order:

Opinion	Size	Age	Shape	Colour	Origin	Material	Noun
beautiful		new		black	Italian		handbag
	large		square	green		glass	fish tank

1 **Complete the sentences by putting the adjectives in the correct order.**

1 The film was a(n) ____boring, old, American____ (American / boring / old) movie.

2 My best friend is a(n) _____ (English / slim / young) girl.

3 Our teacher is a(n) _____ (blonde / attractive / tall) woman.

4 The chairs in our living room are _____ (large / old / leather) armchairs.

5 His birthday present was a(n) _____ (cotton / black / cool) T-shirt.

6 Our kitchen has _____ (orange / wooden / stylish) furniture.

7 They have moved to a(n) _____ (stone / old / enormous) house in France.

8 She has decorated her bag with _____ (round / small / colourful / Indian) beads.

9 Everybody says he's a(n) _____ (young / foreign / intelligent) student.

10 Can you pass me that _____ (green / English / thick) book, please?

Verbs with adjectives

We use adjectives instead of adverbs after some verbs:

* *be, become, get, seem*
  I **am** exhausted.
  He's **become** lazy.
  The baby **gets** tired in the afternoons.
  You **seem** bored with this exercise!

* *feel, look, smell, sound, taste*
  I **feel** happy today.
  You **look** excited.
  The **dinner** smells good.
  That music **sounds** terrible!
  It **tastes** wonderful!

2 **Complete the sentences with the adjectives from the box.**

> awful   boring   delicious   disgusting
> excited   interesting   ~~pleased~~   sad

1 Mum isn't very _____pleased_____ with me because I didn't help her today.

2 The book I'm reading now has become _____ – I'm not going to finish it.

3 Charlie gets _____ when he sees presents. He loves them!

4 Her singing sounds _____ – just like a cat screeching!

5 Your parents seem really _____ . I'd like to meet them again soon.

6 This food you've made tastes _____ – you must give me the recipe.

7 Whenever I see Mike, he always seems _____ . I've never seen him smile.

8 I'm not going to eat this cheese. It smells _____ .

3 **Circle the correct answer.**

1 I can't listen to this music. It *listens /* (*sounds*) terrible.

2 Are you feeling *please / pleased* with yourself?

3 The roses you bought me smell *lovely / tasty.*

4 You must be *careful / carefully* when you go out at night.

5 The film got more *bored / boring* as time went on.

6 She doesn't *seem / be* very impressed with the new teacher.

7 All the students look *tiredly / tired* after their exams last week.

8 We're getting *thirst / thirsty* now – let's have some water.

Adverbs of manner: regular

Adverbs of manner show us the way in which something is done. They answer the question *how?*

(How does he drive?) *He drives* **carefully**.
(How does she sing?) *She sings* **beautifully**.

We make most adverbs by adding *-ly* to the end of the adjective.

quick   →   quickly
slow   →   slowly

When the adjective ends in -e, we take off the -e and add *-ly*.

simple   →   simply
gentle   →   gently

When the adjective ends in -l, we add -ly.

beautiful   →   beautifully
careful   →   carefully

When the adjective ends in a consonant and -y, we take off the -y and add *-ily*.

easy   →   easily
happy   →   happily

4 **Complete the sentences with the correct adverb of manner.**

1 She sings ____beautifully____ (beautiful). I think she should sing in the choir.

2 He behaved _____ (stupid) in front of his friends.

3 They shouted _____ (excited) when they saw the famous actor drive past.

4 The boy ate his food _____ (hungry).

5 I wish you would answer my questions _____ (sensible).

6 He always makes decisions _____ (quick) and I never do.

7 The cats ran _____ (wild) round the garden.

8 He walks _____ (normal) even though he's got his leg in plaster.

Think about it!

Adjectives ending in -e lose the -e and take -ly.

Adverbs of manner: irregular

Some adverbs of manner are irregular.

early   →   early
fast   →   fast
good   →   well
hard   →   hard

high   →   high
late   →   late
near   →   near

5 **Complete the sentences with the adverb form of the adjectives.**

1 He speaks ____politely____ (polite) to everyone he meets.

2 I played very _____ (good) in the school concert.

3 Although he doesn't study _____ (hard), he always gets top marks.

4 He swam _____ (fast) at the Olympics – that's why he won a medal.

5 They live very _____ (cheap) because they grow their own fruit and vegetables.

6 He can jump really _____ (high) – maybe he'll get into the national team!

7 We must arrive at the theatre _____ (early) if we want to get good seats.

8 If you behave _____ (bad), you won't have any friends.

Adverbs of degree

We use the words *enough, quite, too* and *very* to show degree.

- adjective + *enough* + infinitive with *to*
  She isn't **old enough to walk** home from school alone.

- *quite* + adjective
  She's **quite young**, so her mother collects her from school.

- *too* + adjective + infinitive with *to*
  She's **too young** to walk home from school alone.

- *very* + adjective
  She's **very young**, so she can't walk home from school alone.

Notes

We can use *really* instead of *very*.
She's **very** young.
She's **really** young.

6 **Circle the correct answer.**

1   He is a racing driver, so he drives (*very*)/ *enough* fast.

2   I don't think he's *quite / very* good-looking.

3   I'm not tall *quite / enough* to reach that shelf.

4   I wish I was rich *very / enough* to live there.

5   She's *too / very* rude to everybody – I don't like her!

6   I'm *quite / too* hungry – I think I'll have a sandwich.

7   I can't wear this jumper – it's *quite / too* big!

8   It is warm *enough / really* to go for a swim today.

7 **Write sentences with *enough, quite, too* and *very*.**

1   he / be / a good / footballer
    He's quite a good footballer.

2   Donna / be / young / go out alone at night

3   it / not be / hot / go swimming

4   I / be / tired. I am going to bed.

5   they / be / good / but not fantastic

6   the children / not be / old / watch / scary films

Adverbs of place and time

Adverbs of place answer the question *where?*
(Where is she going?) *She is going* **to the park**.
(Where are your parents?) *They are* **at work**.

Adverbs of time answer the question *when?*
(When did you see her?) *I saw her* **yesterday**.
(When will you be home?) *I'll be home* **later this afternoon**.

Notes

Adverbs of place and time usually go at the end of the sentence.

8 **Write the words in the correct order.**

1 you / do / day / come / every / here / ?

   Do you come here every day?

2 at the gym / yesterday / exercised / we

   _____

3 working / tomorrow / will be / all the students / hard / in class

   _____

4 laughed / the children / happily / in the playground

   _____

5 we / the party / last night / leave / had to / early

   _____

6 in London / this plane / will arrive / in the evening

   _____

Comparative and superlative of adjectives

Adjective	Comparative	Superlative
long	longer	the longest
rich	richer	the richest
nice	nicer	the nicest
large	larger	the largest
big	bigger	the biggest
hot	hotter	the hottest
pretty	prettier	the prettiest
happy	happier	the happiest
intelligent	more intelligent	the most intelligent
beautiful	more beautiful	the most beautiful

We use the comparative when we compare two people or things.
*I am **older than** him.*
*She is **more intelligent than** me.*

We use the superlative when we compare one person or thing with others.
*She is **the oldest** member of our family.*
*He is **the most intelligent** person I know.*

Some adjectives are irregular and form their comparative and superlative in a different way to those in the table on the previous page.

good	→	*better*	→	*the best*
bad	→	*worse*	→	*the worst*
much	→	*more*	→	*the most*
little	→	*less*	→	*the least*
far	→	*farther/further*	→	*the farthest/furthest*

9 **Complete the sentences with the comparative or superlative form of the adjectives.**

1   This is _____the most boring_____ (boring) book in the library.
2   What do you think is _____ (pretty) than that picture?
3   Gregory is _____ (careful) than me when he does his homework.
4   You're _____ (dirty) boy I've ever seen!
5   I think English is _____ (easy) than German.
6   My mum is _____ (healthy) than my dad.
7   Maths is _____ (confusing) subject I've ever studied.
8   I've got _____ (little) money in my purse than I thought.

(Not) as ... as

We use *as ... as* when two people or things are similar in some way.
*I am **as clever as** my sister.*
*She is **as tall as** he is.*

We use *not as ... as* when two people or things are different.
*My brother is **not as clever as** my sister.*
*I am **not as tall as** her.*

10   **Write sentences using *(not) as ... as.***

1   these trainers / expensive / my old ones ✗

    <u>These trainers aren't as expensive as my old ones.</u>

2   my sister / tall / my brother ✗

    _____

3   the supermarket / busy / the bakery ✔

    _____

4   these jeans / expensive / those trousers ✔

    _____

5   your brother / naughty / mine ✔

    _____

6   my laptop / good / your computer ✗

    _____

7   their car / fast / as ours ✗

    _____

8   chocolate ice cream / sweet / strawberry ice cream ✔

    _____

Comparison of adverbs

When an adverb has the same form as the adjective, we usually add *-er* to make the comparative and *-est* to make the superlative.

early	→	earlier	→ the earliest
late	→	later	→ the latest

When an adverb ends in *-ly*, we use *more* to make the comparative and *most* to make the superlative.

quickly	→	more quickly	→ the most quickly
carefully	→	more carefully	→ the most carefully

Some adverbs have irregular comparatives and superlatives.

badly	→	worse	→ the worst
far	→	farther/further	→ the farthest/furthest
little	→	less	→ the least
much	→	more	→ the most
well	→	better	→ the best

Notes

We can use *(not) as ... as* with adverbs as well as with adjectives.

*She cooks **as well as** her mother does.*

*He doesn't drive **as well as** his dad.*

11 **Circle the correct answer.**

1   Did you arrive at the lesson ___ than your friend today?

    a   earliest   b   more early   (c)   earlier

2   Mum doesn't sleep ___ as Dad.

    a   as good   b   not as well   c   as well

3   Listening to my English teacher is ___ than writing essays!

    a   most interesting   b   least interesting   c   more interesting

4   Nobody works ___ my mother.

    a   as hard as   b   harder as   c   as harder as

5   My friend Leni talks ___ than anybody I know.

    a   the fastest   b   faster   c   fastest

6   The cats are fighting ___ a pair of lions.

    a   more wildly than   b   wilder than   c   the most wildly of

7   You should eat your food ___ or you will get a tummy ache.

    a   least quickly   b   less quickly   c   the less quickly

8   He speaks French as ___ as he speaks English.

    a   badly   b   bad   c   more bad

Pairwork

Work in pairs. Take turns to talk about how well you and your family/friends can do the activities below.

- play a musical instrument
- speak English
- sing
- dance
- cook
- run

For example:

I can play the guitar better than my best friend.

Writing

Write a description of the people in your class using adverbs and adjectives as much as possible and including comparative and superlative forms.

My teacher is the oldest person in the class and she can speak English better than anyone else.

1 **Complete with the sentences with the verb in brackets. Use the past simple, past continuous or past perfect simple.**

1 I wish I ____was lying____ (lie) on a beach instead of doing homework right now!

2 I wish I _____ (like) fruit as much as you do.

3 If only I _____ (buy) a new computer before this one broke down.

4 If only she _____ (not say) such horrible things to me; we would still be friends.

5 They wish they _____ (be) on holiday today.

6 He wishes he _____ (be) in a different place and not in the library.

7 I wish I _____ (can) play the guitar.

8 We all wish we _____ (study) harder for the exam we took this morning!

2 **Circle the correct answer.**

1 If only you ___ stop doing that!

   a   will   (b) would   c   were

2 He wishes he ___ all those chips!

   a   ate   b   wasn't eating   c   hadn't eaten

3 Don't you sometimes wish you ___ taller?

   a   were   b   was   c   had been

4 Right now he wishes he was ___ !

   a   am sleeping   b   sleeping   c   had been sleeping

5 I wish you ___ more to help me in the house!

   a   were doing   b   will do   c   would do

6 If only you ___ me that sooner.

   a   will tell   b   had told   c   did tell

7 Dad wishes I ___ so much television.

   a   wouldn't watch   b   was watching   c   had watched

8 Do you wish you ___ born in a different century?

   a   was   b   had   c   had been

3 **Find the mistakes in the sentences. Then write them correctly.**

1 I wish I <u>had been</u> fitter.

   <u>I wish I was fitter.</u>

2 Do you ever wish you chosen to learn a different language?

   _____

3 If only you booked the holiday earlier; the hotels wouldn't all be full.

   _____

4 He wishes he hadn't been being so rude.

   _____

5 I really wish you would be stopping making so much noise!

   _____

6 Dad wishes it will rain so he won't have to water the garden.

   _____

4 **Rewrite the sentences in reported speech.**

1   'I was sleeping when you rang,' said Diana.

Diana said _____ she had been sleeping when you rang _____ .

2   'I'll go to the supermarket tomorrow,' said Emily.

Emily said _____ .

3   'We're having chicken for supper this evening,' said Mum.

Mum said _____ .

4   'I must get a present for my aunt,' said Adrian.

Adrian said _____ .

5   'I play tennis every Tuesday evening,' said Simon.

Simon said _____ .

6   'I have been working very hard today,' said Aki.

Aki said _____ .

5 **Circle the correct answer.**

1   Dad said he ___ help me with my homework.

   a   would   b   will   c   can

2   Hector said he ___ watching TV when the earthquake happened.

   a   was   b   had been   c   would be

3   Maria told me she ___ have extra English lessons.

   a   has to   b   had to   c   was

4   I told Mum I ___ to use my savings to buy some new clothes.

   a   would   b   am going   c   was going

5   My friend said he ___ all about computers.

   a   knows   b   knew   c   was knowing

6   Chris said he ___ for me for an hour.

   a   was waiting   b   did wait   c   had been waiting

7   I told the teacher I ___ feeling ill, so I couldn't do the test.

   a   was   b   been   c   were

8   They said they ___ visit us one day.

   a   will   b   can   c   would

6 **Find the extra word and write it in the space.**

1   Mum told <u>to</u> me that she had a headache. _____ to _____

2   My dad told me he had loved me. _____

3   I was surprised when Anna said me she was going on holiday. _____

4   Oleg said he had done his homework by nine o'clock the last evening before. _____

5   She said her friend was to coming to collect her from school. _____

6   Our teacher told us that she had been read all our work. _____

7   Georgia said she was had got lost in the centre of New York. _____

8   He said he'd bought his bike the previous year ago. _____

7 **Rewrite the questions in reported speech.**

1 'When will you be home this evening?' asked her mum.

   Her mum asked when she would be home that evening.

2 'Why do you like football so much?' asked the coach.

   _____

3 'Are you going out on Saturday?' he asked.

   _____

4 'Why has she been studying so much?' asked Tomek.

   _____

5 'How did you make this cake?' Tracy asked.

   _____

6 'Can you give me a lift to school?' he asked my dad.

   _____

7 'Has she finished her project yet?' Satomi asked.

   _____

8 'Why were you so angry?' asked Nick.

   _____

8 **Circle the correct answer.**

1 I asked the boys ___ they were going to play basketball.

   a when   b whether   c what

2 We asked the police officer where the station ___ .

   a be   b is   c was

3 My friend asked me if I ___ to help him.

   a have wanted   b wanted   c did want

4 I asked the racing driver if he ___ how to drive when he was young.

   a has learnt   b had learnt   c was learning

5 The doctor asked me ___ last eaten anything.

   a when I had   b when had I   c when have I

6 The teacher asked me if I ___ all right.

   a am feeling   b feel   c was feeling

7 I asked him ___ tell me his name and address.

   a whether   b if   c to

8 Mum told me ___ spend too long out in the sun.

   a not to   b to not   c not

9 **Circle the correct answer.**

1 He's a(n) ___ man.

a old, tall, Chinese   b tall, old, Chinese   c old, Chinese, tall

2 You seem ___ about the fact that I'm not speaking to him.

a surprising   b surprisingly   c surprised

3 The girls ran ___ up the road.

a quickly   b quickest   c quick

4 The baby plays ___ with her toys for hours.

a happy   b happily   c happly

5 Maybe you didn't read the instructions for your new laptop ___ .

a carefully enough   b enough carefully   c more carefully

6 Who do you know who's ___ me?

a more nicer than   b nicer as   c nicer than

7 I didn't know you could run so ___ !

a faster   b fast   c fastly

8 Do these jeans look ___ the others I've tried on?

a good as   b as good than   c as good as

10 **Complete the sentences with the words from the box.**

> better   comfortable   earlier   more   ~~not~~   simply   the   well

1 My computer's _____not_____ as old as yours.

2 Is there anyone who plays the guitar _____ than you?

3 I think my horse can run _____ quickly than yours.

4 That boy plays football _____ most skillfully on the team.

5 Who else can make lasagna as _____ as your mother?

6 Can you explain this to me _____ ?

7 This is the most _____ bed I've ever slept in!

8 I arrived _____ than the teacher today.

11 **Find the mistakes in the sentences. Then write them correctly.**

1 Sara speaks English the <u>more</u> fluently of all the students.

   Sara speaks English the most fluently of all the students.

2 This is the worse film I've ever seen!

3 You don't seem as tall than your brother.

4 My mum says you should behave nice when you are a guest.

5 He is too much young to ride a motorbike.

6 Mum has got many books than Dad.

Relative clauses

Relative clauses

Relative clauses give us more information about the person, animal or thing we are talking about. Relative clauses begin with a relative pronoun.

We use:

- *who* to talk about people.
  *Mrs Williams is the person **who** teaches English at my college.*

- *whose* to say that something belongs to someone.
  *He's the man **whose** house we bought.*

- *where* to talk about places.
  *This is the hospital **where** my brother was born.*

- *when* to talk about time.
  *2008 was the year **when** my parents first met.*

- *which* to talk about animals or things.
  *This is the grammar book **which** I bought last week.*
  *Where's the cat **which** chases dogs?*

This is the house which I used to live in and these are the people whose grandchildren I played with when I was younger.

Think about it!

You can use *which* or *that* to talk about animals.

1 **Complete the sentences with *who* or *whose*.**

1   The doctor _____who_____ saw Fabian in hospital yesterday was very helpful.

2   Is that the man _____ took your bag?

3   I only know one person _____ name is Quin.

4   Michelangelo was the artist _____ painted the ceiling of the Sistine Chapel.

5   Do you know _____ wallet this is?

6   Where's the teacher _____ is in charge of this class?

7   That's the woman _____ job it is to teach physics.

8   I'm going to visit the boy _____ broke his leg at the gym last week.

2 **Match 1–5 with a–e.**

1   Is this the student   a   who got the best marks this term.

2   Shakespeare is a writer   b   whose work you copied?

3   Are they the children   c   who make bread.

4   Malcolm is the student   d   who broke the window?

5   Bakers are people   e   whose plays are still read today.

3 **Complete the sentences with *which* or *where*.**

1   There's a volcano _____which_____ still erupts in Italy.

2   I've visited an island _____ rare birds live.

3   He saw a cat _____ was as big as a dog.

4   I know a place _____ you can buy excellent cakes.

5   A laptop is a computer _____ you can carry around with you.

6   Mum's looking for a nice place _____ we can go for a picnic.

7   I prefer the trainers _____ have got blue laces.

8   This is the only class in _____ you can listen to music while you work.

4 **Circle the correct answer.**

1 We had a great time last summer *when* / *where* we were on holiday.

2 Why did you choose a dress *where* / *which* doesn't suit you?

3 Do you remember *where* / *when* we were young and we played with toys?

4 My best friend is the person *who* / *whose* advice I listen to the most.

5 I feel happy for children *when* / *whose* grandparents live close by.

6 Have you met the man *whose* / *who* owns the new fast food restaurant in town?

7 Those are the apartments *where* / *which* we stayed last time we were here.

8 I know lots of people *which* / *who* can play the guitar.

5 **Join the two sentences.**

1 There's the hotel. We stayed there last month.

   There's the hotel where we stayed last month.

2 Who was the Greek poet? He wrote *The Iliad.*

   _____

3 I've got a great English teacher. Her name is Mrs Henderson.

   _____

4 It was very hot one year. We were at the beach then.

   _____

5 We've got a new electric car. It's very quiet.

   _____

6 This is the woman. She can speak six languages.

   _____

7 They live in a big house. It has got a beautiful garden.

   _____

8 Can you see the mountain? It is the highest on the island.

   _____

Defining relative clauses

We use defining relative clauses to give essential information about the animal, person or thing we are talking about. Without the information in a defining relative clause, the sentence would not make sense. We do not use commas in this type of clause.

*She's the girl **who** has a new bike.*
*We stayed in a hotel **which** was built out of marble.*
*He's the man **whose** wife has won the lottery.*

Notes

In defining relative clauses, we can use *that* instead of *who* and *which*.
*There's the house **which** my uncle built.*
*There's the house **that** my uncle built.*

We do not need to use the relative pronouns *who*, *which* and *that* when they are the object of the defining relative clause.
*Here's the shoe shop **which** Kim likes.*
Here's the shoe shop Kim likes.

6 **Circle the correct answer.**

1   Where's the girl ___ has lost her notebook?
    a   what   b   whose   c   who

2   I'm wearing the bracelet ___ you bought me for my birthday.
    a   when   b   –   c   who

3   Where are the photos ___ you took last weekend?
    a   that   b   when   c   where

4   She's the girl ___ Kostas sits next to.
    a   whose   b   what   c   who

5   I've met a man ___ brother is a famous actor.
    a   who   b   –   c   whose

6   John's been promoted to manager at the office ___ he works.
    a   –   b   where   c   which

7   This is the place ___ I was telling you about.
    a   –   b   what   c   where

8   Where are the keys ___ open the door?
    a   who   b   which   c   what

7 **Match 1–6 with a–f.**

1   The airport where we're landing   a   that tells us what words mean.
2   Do you know anybody   b   is my brother.
3   The young man who's got a moustache   c   who can repair computers?
4   A dictionary is a thing   d   who robbed the local bank.
5   The pyramids were built by people   e   hasn't got many shops.
6   The police have caught the man   f   who lived a very long time ago.

Non-defining relative clauses

We use non-defining relative clauses to give extra information about the person, animal or thing we are talking about. This information is not essential to the meaning of the sentence. Non-defining relative clauses are separated from the main sentence by commas.

My mum's best friend, **who is a nurse,** *lives next door to us.*
London, **which is the capital of England,** *is a fascinating city.*

Notes

We cannot leave the relative pronoun out of a non-defining relative clause.
My red jacket, **which I bought in the sales last year,** *is too small for me now.*

We cannot use *that* instead of *who* or *which* in a non-defining relative clause.
The City Hotel, **which has got two hundred rooms,** *opened last week.*

8 **Write *D* for defining relative clause and *N* for non-defining relative clause.**

1   I found the books which you left on your desk. _D_

2   I really like my friend's sister, whose name is Misty. ___

3   Do you remember the place where we went for our first holiday? ___

4   The Blue Lagoon, which is in Iceland, is a popular tourist attraction. ___

5   Have you still got the shirt that I gave you for your birthday? ___

6   That singer, who once gave me his autograph, is really talented. ___

7   I think that's the man whose cat ran away. ___

8   I've read a book about Neil Armstrong, who was the first man to walk on the moon. ___

9   Isn't 2015 the year when we went on holiday to Holland? ___

10 The boys over there, who are making a noise, are always getting into trouble. ___

9 Add commas where necessary.

1 My best friend, who goes to our school, is leaving next month.

2 The Natural History Museum where there are models of dinosaurs is a good place to take children.

3 *The Sunflowers* was painted by an artist whose name was Vincent Van Gogh.

4 J K Rowling is the author whose books are read in many countries.

5 My father's mother who lived to be 99 was only 1.40 metres tall.

6 People who have to watch their weight shouldn't eat a lot of cakes.

7 There was a huge traffic jam when we decided to travel into town yesterday.

8 George is the boy in the photograph who is holding the kitten.

9 This coffee shop opened last month when I was on holiday.

10 My old school which is 100 years old was closed in September.

10 Match 1–8 with a–h.

1	Bunk beds are beds	a	when life was hard for many people.
2	He is a rock singer	b	where the Camp Nou stadium is.
3	Astronauts are people	c	which are on top of each other.
4	Architects are people	d	which is eaten in many eastern countries.
5	Rice is a food	e	who design buildings.
6	Barcelona is the place	f	who travel into space.
7	The nineteenth century was a time	g	who writes songs about life in the USA.
8	She is an actor	h	whose films are very popular.

11 **Tick (✔) the correct sentence, *a* or *b*.**

1   a   Those tablets, which are very popular, are still expensive. ✔
    b   Those tablets which are popular are still expensive. ___

2   a   I'm really glad I've got a friend who can fix computers. ___
    b   I'm really glad I've got a friend, who can fix computers. ___

3   a   The Mediterranean diet, what includes a lot of olive oil, is very healthy. ___
    b   The Mediterranean diet, which includes a lot of olive oil, is very healthy. ___

4   a   In the nineteenth century, where Victoria was Queen of England, people worked hard. ___
    b   In the nineteenth century, when Victoria was Queen of England, people worked hard. ___

5   a   Oleg is the boy who was at the party yesterday. ___
    b   Oleg is the boy who he was at the party yesterday. ___

6   a   Loch Ness is the place in Scotland which people say they have seen a monster. ___
    b   Loch Ness is the place in Scotland where people say they have seen a monster. ___

12 **Complete the text by writing one word in each gap.**

I went out yesterday with my friend Mark. He's the boy ¹ _____who_____ I'm going to play tennis with next week. We went with my parents to a town ² _____ is called Hilltown, not far from where we live. The first shop we went to was a place ³ _____ they make great cakes. We wanted to buy one ⁴ _____ was special. I wanted a cake made of chocolate, but the baker ⁵ _____ owns that bakery said he didn't have any chocolate cakes. He told us he had a friend ⁶ _____ makes the best chocolate cakes and he would find out ⁷ _____ he was going to make them again. After we'd done a bit of shopping, we went to visit Mark's grandmother, ⁸ _____ lives near Hilltown. Her flat, ⁹ _____ is small but very nice, is next to the park ¹⁰ _____ Mark and I first played tennis together. At half past eight, ¹¹ _____ we realised how late it was, we said goodbye to Mark's grandmother and went home. We stopped for a pizza at the café ¹² _____ is owned by Mark's cousin and we arrived home at ten o'clock.

13 **Find the extra word and write it in the space.**

1   Our neighbours, who ~~they~~ don't like animals, shout at our dog. _____they_____

2   This is the book which who I've been reading for the last three weeks. _____

3   The hospital in where I was born has been closed down. _____

4   Chocolate, which is my favourite food, that is fattening if you eat a lot of it. _____

5   My friend Louise, whose dress which I've borrowed, is exactly the same size as me. _____

6   What's the name of that rock group whose which your brother listens to all the time? _____

7   Where is the kitten what which you found? _____

8   Fruit and vegetables, which they contain lots of vitamins, are good for your skin. _____

14 **Complete the sentences with a relative clause and your own words.**

1 My mother is a person _____ *who I love very much.* _____

2 I know a boy _____ .

3 Italy is a country _____ .

4 I've seen a film _____ .

5 A computer is a thing _____ .

6 I don't know anybody _____ .

Pairwork

Work in pairs. Take turns to talk about people you know using relative clauses.

For example:
Mrs Thomson is the woman **who** *lives next door to my grandmother.*
Andrew is the man **whose** *house is behind mine.*

Writing

Write an email to your friend in England telling them about the town where you live. Think about the points below.

- the buildings (where they are, what they are for)
- the shops (what you can buy there, who owns them)
- people (who they are, what they do, where they live)
- any other things in your town that you think are interesting

Gerunds

Gerunds are verbs with the *-ing* ending.
*study**ing***
*danc**ing***
*learn**ing***

We use gerunds:

- as nouns.
  *They love **walking**.*
  *I hate **running**.*
  *My brother enjoys **building**.*

- as the subject of a sentence.
  ***Sailing** is my favourite hobby.*
  ***Studying** is not something I enjoy.*

- after prepositions.
  *I'm not good at **skiing**.*
  *We're looking forward to **seeing** you soon.*

- after the verb *go* when we are talking about sports.
  *I hope we go **snowboarding** this winter.*

- after some verbs and phrases.
  admit
  be used to
  deny
  can't help
  can't stand
  dislike
  (don't) mind
  enjoy
  feel like
  finish
  hate
  imagine
  keep
  like
  love
  miss
  practise
  spend time

*I **don't mind doing** the washing up.*
***Keep walking** in that direction.*
*They **love swimming** in the sea.*

I'm really good at cooking. I think I'll start taking cooking classes.

Maybe you should try doing a short course first in case you don't like it.

1 **Complete the sentences with gerunds.**

1   Kya's really good at _____learning_____ (learn) new languages.

2   _____ (train) for the Olympics is really hard work.

3   Thanks for _____ (help) me to fix my bike.

4   I love _____ (make) breakfast for my family at the weekends.

5   I've just read an interesting book about _____ (exercise) your brain!

6   I'm interested in _____ (get) a new computer.

7   My friend hates _____ (spend) a lot of money on clothes.

8   If you go _____ (swim) later, I want to come as well.

9   There's no point in _____ (tell) him what to do. He never listens!

10 _____ (eat) too much sugar is not good for you.

2 **Write sentences.**

1   my brother / hate / get up / early

My brother hates getting up early. _____

2   I / enjoy / meet / new friends

_____

3   she / not mind / get up / early

_____

4   you / spend / hours / listen / to music / ?

_____

5   how often / do you go / ski / ?

_____

6   I / enjoy / receive / presents

_____

7   they / be used to / eat / spicy food

_____

8   we / not feel like / go out / tonight

_____

3 **Complete the sentences with the verbs from the box. Use gerunds.**

| do   eat   go   help   hit   laugh   listen   play   speak   steal |

1   My sister can't stand _____eating_____ mushrooms.

2   I feel like _____ to watch a football match.

3   If you don't practise _____ English, you won't pass your oral exam.

4   A lot of people enjoy _____ to music.

5   The girl admitted _____ the money but denied _____ her friend.

6   I don't mind _____ you with your homework, but I can't stand _____ maths!

7   He tells such funny jokes that I can't help _____ when I talk to him.

8   She should practise _____ the piano more if she wants to become a musician.

Infinitives after verbs

We make infinitives by adding *to* to the verb.
to see
to wonder
to search

Some verbs are followed by the infinitive:

afford	*need*
allow	*offer*
arrange	*persuade*
ask	*plan*
decide	*promise*
hope	*refuse*
invite	*want*
learn	*would like*
manage	

*I'm allowed **to stay** out until midnight on Saturdays.*
*He needs **to see** a doctor.*
*We persuaded her **to tell** the truth.*

4 **Write sentences with the verbs from the box. Use infinitives.**

~~buy~~	give	learn	leave	meet	take	tidy	win

1   Frank / want / me / a book / at the bookshop
    Frank wanted to buy me a book at the bookshop.

2   I / decide / Spanish / last year
    _____

3   I / refuse / my room
    _____

4   the teacher / promise / me / extra lessons
    _____

5   I / plan / home / when I'm 21
    _____

6   they / hope / the lottery
    _____

7   we / arrange / outside the cinema / at eight o'clock
    _____

8   Lily / ask / Vicky / her brother / to school
    _____

Infinitives after adjectives

Some adjectives are followed by the infinitive:

amazed	*glad*	*sad*	*surprised*
fascinated	*happy*	*sorry*	*wonderful*

I'm **happy to hear** that you got the job.
She was **glad to be** chosen for the team.
It's **wonderful to be** here.

Notes

We use the infinitive with the words *too* and *enough*.
It's **too** hot **to go out** for a walk.
It's **not** cool **enough to go out** for a walk.

Think about it!

Too cold and *not hot enough* have the same meaning.

5 **Complete the sentences with the words from the box.**

> enough   lazy   sad   surprised   to (x2)   ~~too~~   wonderful

1 She's _____ too _____ tired to work.

2 We were _____ to hear the news.

3 The fridge isn't cold _____ to keep the ice cream frozen.

4 I was sorry _____ hear that you have been ill.

5 Is he clever enough _____ understand the physics lesson?

6 It was _____ to see our grandparents after such a long time.

7 All the children were very _____ to hear that the TV was broken.

8 He's too _____ to do any homework.

6 **Circle the correct answer.**

1 His parents persuaded Boris (not to leave) / not leaving school.

2 He keeps *to tell / telling* me he is coming.

3 Did you manage *to get / getting* the day off school yesterday?

4 How did you learn *doing / to do* such good card tricks?

5 I don't feel like *to eat / eating* pizza tonight.

6 Why don't we offer *to help / helping* Dad do the cooking?

7 He decided *to move / moving* to the USA.

8 Do you miss *seeing / to see* your grandparents every day?

7 **Complete the sentences with gerunds or infinitives.**

1 We don't want _____ to do _____ (do) anything today except lie on the beach!

2 Our visitors aren't used to _____ (eat) so much bread with their meals.

3 Can you imagine _____ (see) a ghost?

4 She promised _____ (behave) well at the restaurant.

5 I wish my family could afford _____ (go) on holiday to Australia.

6 Mum can't stand _____ (see) people throwing rubbish in the street.

7 What do you hope _____ (be) when you're older?

8 I want to spend some time _____ (relax) this summer.

Gerund or infinitive?

Some verbs can be followed by the gerund or the infinitive without a change in meaning:

- *begin, continue, hate, like, start*
  They **began studying** at nine o'clock.
  They **began to study** at nine o'clock.
  The footballers **continued playing**.
  The footballers **continued to play**.
  We **hate travelling** by bus.
  We **hate to travel** by bus.
  I **like walking** in the rain.
  I **like to walk** in the rain.
  The choir **started to sing**.
  The choir **started singing**.

Some other verbs can also be followed by the gerund or the infinitive, but there is a change in meaning:

- *forget, go on, regret, remember, stop, try*
  I **forgot to go** to my piano class. (I didn't remember, so I didn't go.)
  I **forgot being** at that piano class. (I had no memory of being in the piano class.)
  The teacher **went on to talk** about other subjects. (The teacher changed the topic of his lesson.)
  The speaker **went on talking** for two hours. (The teacher spoke about the same topic.)
  I **regret to tell** you that you did not pass the test. (I'm sorry to give this news.)
  I **regret telling** you my secret because you told everyone else. (I wish I hadn't told you.)
  I **remembered to lock** the door this morning. (I didn't forget.)
  I think I **remember locking** the door this morning, but I'm not sure. (I have the memory of it.)
  They **stopped to get** some petrol. (They stopped one unmentioned activity, e.g. driving, to get petrol.)
  They **stopped driving**. (They stopped the mentioned activity.)
  Try adding salt to the soup if it is tasteless. (Adding salt might make the soup taste better.)
  Try to take the milk to her without spilling it. (You may not be able to do it, but you should try to do it.)

8 **Complete the sentences with the verbs from the box in the correct form.**

> continue   ~~go on~~   hate   like   regret
> remember   try (x2)

1   I can't _____ go on _____ studying all night!

2   Have you ever _____ to understand Japanese?

3   They _____ to leave their pet alone when they go out for the day.

4   Did you _____ to close all the windows before you left the house?

5   I _____ not studying for my exams as I failed them.

6   Do you _____ eating Chinese food? It's delicious.

7   If you can't do the exercise, _____ asking a friend to help you.

8   The students _____ working after the break.

9 **Tick (✔) the correct sentence, _a_ or _b_.**

1   a   I stopped to talk and started listening to the teacher. ___
    b   I stopped talking and started listening to the teacher. ✔

2   a   I enjoy watching television at the weekends. ___
    b   I enjoy to watch television at the weekends. ___

3   a   We regret telling you that you did not pass the test. ___
    b   We regret to tell you that you did not pass the test. ___

4   a   Naysha joined the team two years ago and soon went on becoming the captain. ___
    b   Naysha joined the team two years ago and soon went on to become the captain. ___

5   a   I forgot to turn off the oven! ___
    b   I forgot turn off the oven! ___

6   a   I don't remember to say that! ___
    b   I don't remember saying that! ___

7   a   Did he deny to take books? ___
    b   Did he deny taking the books? ___

8   a   I'd like to see the Grand Canyon. ___
    b   I'd like seeing the Grand Canyon. ___

10 **Find the mistakes in the sentences. Then write them correctly.**

1 It's really good to <u>seeing</u> you again.

   It's really good to see you again.

2 I offered going with him, but he said 'no'.

3 Mum can't afford buy herself a new car at the moment.

4 They stopped to talk when the teacher came in.

5 I need practising writing essays so I can pass my English exam.

6 We've arranged meeting at nine o'clock in the library.

11 **Complete the text by writing one word in each gap.**

I had a wonderful time last weekend. I had wanted ¹ _____to_____ stay at my friend's
house for ages and my mum finally said I was ² _____ to go. When I arrived, we felt
³ _____ having something to eat. My friend can't ⁴ _____ meat and I hate
vegetables, so it was a while before we decided what ⁵ _____ have! In the end, we
agreed to ⁶ _____ spaghetti with a cheese sauce. My friend had arranged for us to
⁷ _____ to the ice rink in the afternoon. She'd promised to ⁸ _____ me
how to skate. I loved it – even though I couldn't ⁹ _____ falling over all the time!
I can't imagine ever being good ¹⁰ _____ ice skating. In the evening, we had planned
to ¹¹ _____ a nice meal for my friend's mum and dad, so we had to start searching
for recipes again! Anyway, we managed to ¹² _____ a nice recipe and we all enjoyed
our dinner together. I'd forgotten to take a good book to read in bed, but my friend lent me one
of her books, which was great because I'm not ¹³ _____ to going to sleep without
¹⁴ _____ in bed first. I had a really brilliant weekend and when it was time for me to
go, we promised to see each other again very soon.

12 **Complete the sentences using gerunds or infinitives and your own words.**

1   I think I will continue _____ to go to the ice rink every Saturday _____ .

2   My friend promised _____ .

3   I'm not used to _____ .

4   I like to spend time _____ .

5   I'm not strong enough _____ .

6   I need _____ .

7   I'm too lazy _____ .

8   I'm going to ask the teacher _____ .

Pairwork

Work in pairs. Take turns to ask and answer questions using verbs from this unit. Use the gerund and the infinitive.

For example:

What can't you stand doing on Saturdays?

What have you refused to do this week?

What do you dislike eating the most?

Writing

Write a report for your English teacher about what you did last weekend. Remember to say what you liked, didn't like, enjoyed, hated, etc. as well as saying something about your general likes and dislikes. Use as many gerunds and infinitives as you can.

Causative

Tense	Example
Present simple	I have my car washed every month.
Present continuous	She is having her hair cut at the moment.
Past simple	We had our house repainted last year.
Past continuous	They were having their washing machine repaired.
Present perfect simple	We have had the windows cleaned.
Present perfect continuous	We have been having the house decorated.
Past perfect simple	He had already had his bike repaired.
Past perfect continuous	She had been having her kitchen painted.
Future simple	I'll have my hair dyed black!
Future continuous	He will be having his washing machine fixed.
Future perfect simple	They will have had their roof repaired.
be going to	They're going to have the bedroom made bigger.
Modals (present)	We must have the windows washed.

The causative is formed in the following way:
have + object + past participle of the main verb
She **had** her wedding dress **made**.
She isn't **having** her bedroom painted this year.
Has she **had** her eyes **tested** recently?

The object of the sentence must come directly before the past participle of the main verb.

You look really nice!

Thanks! I had my hair cut!

We use the causative:

* to say that someone else has done something for us or on our behalf.
  Karol has mended his watch. (Karol did it himself.)
  *Karol **has had** his watch **mended**.* (Someone else did it for Karol.)

* to describe something unpleasant that has happened.
  *They **had** their bikes **stolen** while they were away.*
  *Malcolm **had** his window **broken**.*

Notes

When we are speaking, we can use the verb *get* instead of *have*.
*He's **getting** his car **repaired** at the moment.*

When we talk about unpleasant events, we cannot use *get* instead of *have*.

1 Write the words in the correct order.

1 have had / they / by email / sent / the school reports
They have had the school reports sent by email.

2 his hair / has had / Andros / cut

3 is going to have / she / her / painted / bedroom

4 to their house / their mum's flowers / delivered / are having / they

5 all the food for the party / are having / by their dad / they / cooked

6 are having / by a professional photographer / they / taken / photographs

2 Complete the sentences with the causative. Use the words in brackets and the present simple or present continuous.

1 She always ___has her clothes made___ (her clothes / make) by a top designer.
2 She _____ (her new coat / clean), so she'll have to wear her old one.
3 My mother _____ (her hair / do) every six weeks.
4 I _____ (a cake / make) for my birthday party.
5 I _____ (my eyes / not test) very often.
6 We _____ (the new bed / not deliver) today because we're going out.

3 **Complete the sentences with the causative. Use the words in brackets and the past simple or past continuous.**

1 He _____was having his hair cut_____ (his hair / cut) when I saw him.

2 I _____ (my computer / repair) last week.

3 He _____ (his bandages / change) by the doctor.

4 We _____ (our homework / check) by the teacher.

5 She _____ (her photo / take) when it started to rain.

6 We _____ (the TV / repair) yesterday, so I watched my favourite programme on my tablet.

7 I _____ (my teeth / check) at the dentist's today.

8 We _____ (the books / deliver) to the school last week.

4 **Write sentences with the causative. Write one sentence with the present perfect and one with the present continuous. Use different time phrases.**

1 (her bike / fixed)

She _hasn't had her bike fixed. She's having_ _it fixed tomorrow_____ .

2 (my project / checked)

I _____

_____ .

3 (her eyes / test)

She _____

_____ .

4 (the house / paint)

Dad _____

_____ .

5 (his shirt / iron)

He _____

_____ .

6 (the window / repaired)

They _____

_____ .

5 **Complete the sentences with the causative. Use the words in brackets and the past perfect simple.**

1 They _____hadn't had their bedroom painted_____ (their bedroom / not paint) for ages.

2 They _____ (the roof / fix) before the winter.

3 The baby _____ (his hearing / test) soon after he was born.

4 He _____ (his tyres / check) before starting the journey.

5 The tourists _____ (their bags / search) before they got on the plane.

6 He _____ (any of his books / not publish) before he was fifty.

7 Her mother _____ (her hair / dye) black.

8 Her friend _____ (a tennis court / build) in her garden.

6 Complete the sentences with the verbs from the box. Use the causative.

> break   build   cook   cut off   ~~steal~~   test

1 She _____had her wallet stolen_____ . (her wallet)
2 They _____ because they didn't pay the bill. (the electricity)
3 He _____ by an expert chef. (his meal)
4 We _____ by a football. (our living room window)
5 The children _____ by their dad. (a tree house)
6 She _____ because she couldn't see very well. (her eyes)

7 Write questions using the causative.

1 the twins / their photo / take / on Saturday / ?
_Did the twins have their photo taken on Saturday?_____

2 Dad / his office / decorate / during the holidays / ?
_____

3 he / flowers / send / to his mum / yesterday / ?
_____

4 your brother / his hair / cut / very short / ?
_____

5 you / your old bike / repair / ?
_____

6 the school / some new tennis courts / build / last year / ?
_____

8 Complete the questions using the causative.

1 You meet someone you know at the optician's.
'Are ___you having your eyes tested___ (your eyes / test)?'
2 You see your dad at the garage.
'Are _____ (the car / wash)?'
3 You visit a friend whose hair is now a different colour.
'When did _____ (your hair / dye)?'
4 You see a friend who is coming out of the dentist's holding her cheek.
'Have _____ (a tooth / take out)?'
5 Your best friend suddenly appears wearing earrings.
'Did _____ (your ears / pierce) yesterday?'
6 The TV isn't working properly.
'When do you think you _____ (the TV / fix)?'

9 **Complete the sentences with the words from the box.**

> ~~going~~   had (x2)   have (x2)   having   sent   were

1   He is _____going_____ to have his hair cut tomorrow.
2   I won't _____ my eyes tested tomorrow because I'm ill.
3   We _____ our tickets changed so we were able to get a later flight.
4   We _____ having our test results announced when the fire alarm went off.
5   We _____ the pizza delivered to Alex's house. It was delicious!
6   The musicians always _____ all their songs recorded at the same studio.
7   The girl had all her party invitations _____ by post.
8   My sister is _____ a special party organised for her birthday.

10 **Read the information and complete the sentences with the verb in brackets. Use the causative.**

> **Think about it!**
>
> Do not forget to put the past participle after the object of the sentence!

A   Your neighbours paid for some home improvements.

1   swimming pool in the garden (put)

Our neighbours _____ had a swimming pool put in the garden _____ .

2   flowers and trees around the house (plant)

They _____ .

3   70-inch TV on the wall (install)

They _____ .

B   You have had your bike fixed.

1   the brakes (check)

I _____ .

2   the tyres (change)

I _____ .

3   the frame (clean)

I _____ .

C   Your friend has had a medical check-up done.

1   her eyes (test)

Samantha _____ .

2   her blood (take)

She _____ .

3   her heart rate (measure)

She _____ .

11 **Complete the sentences in your own words. Use the causative.**

1 Last Saturday morning, _____ I had my hair styled _____ .

2 Yesterday, _____ .

3 Next week, _____ .

4 Tomorrow, _____ .

5 Today, _____ .

6 Every month, _____ .

7 Once a year _____ .

8 Next year, _____ .

Pairwork

Work in pairs. Imagine that you haven't seen each other for a year. Take turns to talk about things that you or your family have had done in the last year.

For example:
We have had our house painted a different colour.
My dad has had his car fixed.

Writing

Write an email to a friend in England, wishing them a happy summer. With the email, you also send him a photo of your house and a photo of your family. Tell your friend what you and your family have had done recently, and ask them about their family. Use the causative as much as possible.

Clauses of reason

We use clauses of reason to explain why something happens. They are introduced by a number of words and phrases.

- *as/since*
  As/Since *I was late for the meeting, I took a taxi.*

- *because*
  *Mum made spaghetti **because** it's my favourite.*

- *the reason for* + noun
  The reason for *his bad behaviour was not clear.*

- *the reason why* + clause
  The reason why *he behaved badly was not clear.*

- *because of* + noun/the fact that
  Because of *his broken toe, he had to stop playing football.*
  Because of the fact that *he had broken his toe, he had to stop playing football.*

- *due to* + noun/the fact that
  Due to *the weather, we couldn't go to the park.*
  Due to the fact that *she had a lot of homework, she couldn't go out with her friends.*

Why are you so happy?

I'm happy because my dad bought me tickets to the concert on Saturday.

That's fantastic. Lucky you!

1 **Complete the sentences with the phrases from the box. There may be more than one possible answer.**

> as   ~~because~~   because of   due to
> since   the reason for   the reason why (x2)

1 _____Because_____ they loved camping, they used to go every year.
2 _____ she left her school was that her dad got a new job.
3 She failed the exam _____ the fact that she hadn't studied hard enough.
4 _____ the cancellation of the flight was the bad weather.
5 They decided to go there for the weekend _____ they had friends there.
6 _____ she didn't come to the party was that she wasn't feeling very well.
7 On holiday, they played lots of games _____ they didn't have any homework to do.
8 _____ the fact that she was a good athlete, she was on all the sports teams.

Clauses of purpose

We use clauses of purpose to explain why someone does something.
They are introduced by a number of words and phrases.

to + infinitive
in order to + infinitive
so that
in case
for

In order to + infinitive is more formal than *to* + infinitive. In negative sentences, we put the word *not* before the word *to*.
*She went to Paris **to study** French.*
*She went to Paris **in order to study** French.*
***In order not to** forget all her English over the holidays, she read lots of books in English.*

So that is followed by a verb in the present simple or *can/could* or *will/would*, depending on the meaning of the sentence.
*Sarah saves her pocket money **so that** she **can** buy clothes with it.*
*I'm going to get up early tomorrow **so that** I **will** have plenty of time to get ready.*

We never use *will* or *would* after *in case* even if we are talking about the future. In this case, we use the present simple or the present continuous.
*Take some extra money **in case** you need it.*

We use a gerund or a noun after the word *for*.
*This knife is **for cutting** meat.*
*We went to a really nice restaurant **for lunch**.*

2 **Circle the correct answer.**

1 I will take some sandwiches with me in case I *will get* / *get* hungry.

2 In order to *having* / *have* more time at the beach, we left home early.

3 He uses his computer for *writing* / *write* all his homework.

4 Let's save up our money so that *to buy* / *we can buy* a new laptop.

5 We'll take money with us in case we *catch* / *to catch* the bus.

6 They went into town in *order* / *case* to go to the shops.

7 Invite lots of people to the party *in case* / *in the case* some people can't come.

8 I decided to ride my bike *to* / *for* get some exercise.

Think about it!

In case does not mean the same as *if* and you cannot use *in case* instead of *if* in conditional sentences.

Clauses of contrast and concession

We use clauses of contrast and concession to show some kind of 'disagreement' in a sentence. They are introduced by a number of words and phrases.

but
although/even though
in spite of/despite + noun/*the fact that/-ing*
however/nevertheless
while/whereas

We bought some jeans, **but** we didn't find any trainers we liked.
Although/Even though the hotel wasn't near the sea, it was very nice.
Despite the heat, they had to try to sleep.
In spite of the fact that the exams were difficult, she thought that she had passed.

In spite of having a bad headache, she had to finish reading the book.
He eats a lot. **However,/Nevertheless,** he isn't fat.
She loved dancing, **while** he didn't like it at all.
This photo shows a castle, **whereas** the other photo is of a tower.
Whereas some of them agreed with him, others didn't.

Notes

We never put *of* after *despite*.
We always put a comma after *however*.

3 Complete the sentences with the words from the box. There may be more than one possible answer.

> although   but   despite   even though
> however   in spite   whereas   while

1 They wanted to make a cake. _____However_____ , there were no eggs in the fridge.
2 I enjoy action films, _____ my sister enjoys comedies.
3 We decided to go out for a walk _____ it was raining.
4 _____ I was very angry with Peter, I still invited him to my party.
5 _____ of the fact that I said I was sorry, he is still angry with me.
6 _____ most people enjoy going to the beach, I hate it.
7 I wanted to go out, _____ the others wanted to stay at home.
8 _____ the heat, we went out for a walk.

4 Complete the sentences.

1 He ran very fast, but he still didn't win the race.
Despite _____ the fact that he ran very fast, he still didn't win the race _____ .
2 He likes meat and his wife likes vegetables.
Whereas he _____ .
3 They felt very tired. They stayed up late talking.
Even though _____ .
4 He was rich and famous, but he wasn't happy.
In spite of _____ .
5 She already had three handbags. She wanted one more!
Although _____ .

5 Circle the correct answer.

1 Take a jumper ___ it gets cold tonight.
   a   so that   b   due to   (c)   in case
2 They went on a picnic ___ the rain.
   a   despite   b   because of   c   in spite
3 Aran likes football, ___ Dominik likes tennis.
   a   in spite of   b   whereas   c   however
4 Because of ___ , the match was cancelled.
   a   raining   b   to rain   c   the rain
5 The reason ___ the mistake is not clear.
   a   why   b   for   c   so
6 ___ she likes meat, she doesn't want roast beef.
   a   Even   b   In spite of   c   Although

Clauses of result

We use clauses of result to talk about the effects of an action. They are introduced by a number of words and phrases.

so
so + adjective/adverb (*that*)
such + (*a*/*an*) adjective + noun (*that*)
as a result
therefore

We missed the bus, **so** *we had to walk home.*
The pizza was **so** *hot* **that** *I couldn't eat it.*
She plays the piano **so** *well* **that** *she has already won lots of prizes.*
It was **such** *a nice day* **that** *we wanted to go for a picnic.*
He failed some of his exams and, **as a result***, he had to take them again in September.*
They lost their tickets for the concert. **Therefore***, they didn't see their favourite singer.*

Notes

We also use:

- *such a lot of* + plural/uncountable noun.
  Molly has **such a lot of** *toys in her bed that she can't lie down.*
  There is **such a lot of** *dust in here that I can't breathe!*

- *so much/little* + uncountable noun.
  There is **so much** *furniture in here that there isn't room to move!*
  He knows **so little** *English that he can't even say hello.*

- *so many/few* + countable noun.
  I've seen **so many** *films like this that I find them boring.*
  She knows **so few** *people that she's lonely.*

---

6 **Complete the sentences with *so* or *such a/an*.**

1 It was _____such a_____ hot day that we spent all day in the sea.

2 There were _____ lot of people at the concert that we could hardly move.

3 They were _____ happy when their first grandchild was born.

4 It was _____ awful film that we left halfway through.

5 There were _____ many people on the bus that we had to stand up all the way.

6 The little boy ran _____ fast that I couldn't catch him.

7 He was _____ good teacher that we all learnt a lot.

8 There were _____ many different kinds of ice cream that we didn't know which one to buy.

7 Rewrite the sentences using the word in bold. Use between two and five words.

1 There were large crowds and we couldn't see the band. **due**

We couldn't see the band _____ due to _____ the large crowds.

2 Although I put lots of sun cream on, I still got burnt. **spite**

I still got burnt, _____ I put lots of sun cream on.

3 My mum baked so many cakes that we were eating them for days! **such**

My mum baked _____ cakes that we were eating them for days!

4 Since he wanted to get good marks in the exams, he studied very hard. **order**

He studied very hard _____ get good marks in the exams.

5 They thought the weather might get cool, so they took jackets with them. **case**

They took jackets with them _____ got cool.

6 She went to the party, despite feeling ill. **though**

She went to the party, _____ ill.

7 We left early because we were bored. **reason**

The _____ early was that we were bored.

8 We missed the bus and so we had to walk home. **result**

We missed the bus and, _____ , we had to walk home.

8 Find the extra word and write it in the space.

1 The reason why <u>for</u> they were happy was that they were on holiday! _____ for _____

2 They got up early, despite of the fact that they hadn't had much sleep. _____

3 There were so such many people at the party that they made a lot of noise. _____

4 There weren't enough chairs, so that we got some from another table. _____

5 They were so kind to us that we said thanked them very much. _____

6 He turned on the television for to listen to the news. _____

7 In spite of he spending all day studying, he still had to study in the evening. _____

8 We went to bed because of we were tired. _____

9 Match 1–8 with a–h.

1 She had a good breakfast every morning.   a they couldn't wait to go on holiday.

2 In order to have some peace and quiet,   b they went to bed early.

3 Since they were tired   c so that Dad could talk on the phone.

4 We turned the music down   d However, she was always hungry again by lunchtime.

5 It was such a bad film   e he was still able to concentrate on his work.

6 You should wear trainers   f that we left the cinema.

7 Despite all the noise,   g in case you have to walk a long way.

8 Although they enjoyed school,   h she went to her room and shut the door.

10 **Complete the text by writing one word in each gap.**

A visit to the zoo

Last Saturday, Jair and Omar didn't have a lot of jobs to do,
[1] _____so_____ they decided to go to the zoo. The zoo is Omar's
favourite place [2] _____ he knows so [3] _____
of the animals and birds there. Jair took his camera in
[4] _____ there were any new animals.

The first place they went to in the zoo was the monkey house.
The monkeys all made so [5] _____ noise that Jair
and Omar couldn't hear themselves speak! They laughed a lot
[6] _____ of all the funny things the monkeys did.

Next, they went to the elephant house, [7] _____ they didn't
stay there long [8] _____ to the terrible smell! They quickly
went outside [9] _____ have a look at the baby elephant
with its mother. Then they had to hurry in order [10] _____
to miss feeding-time for the seals, which were very good at catching
the fish the keepers threw to them! After seeing a few more animals
and lots of colourful birds, it was time to go home.

[11] _____ though Omar was tired, he didn't want to go
home, [12] _____ Jair said, 'Come on, Omar, it's been such
a nice day, but I think I've had enough now.'

11 **Complete the sentences in your own words.**

1   The reason for going to school _____ is to learn as much as possible _____ .

2   I like learning English because _____ .

3   I got up early last week in order to _____ .

4   I always carry _____ with me in case _____ .

5   The reason why I like _____ .

6   Due to the cold/hot weather, I _____ .

7   I should eat lots of fresh fruit so that _____ .

8   Although I live in _____ .

Pairwork

Work in pairs. Plan the main ideas of a descriptive story together. Decide what you are going to describe – a visit to an interesting place, a special holiday, etc. – and talk about what you think your story should be like.

Writing

Using your ideas from the Pairwork exercise above, write a short story. Use as many phrases from the unit as you can. Use your imagination to make the story more interesting.

Last year ...

Although ...

Despite ...

In the end ...

1 Match 1–6 with a–f.

1	Skyscrapers are buildings	a	who like doing exams?
2	Tigers aren't animals	b	with a fascinating history.
3	Bakers are people	c	who is in a rock group.
4	He is a musician	d	which are extremely tall.
5	Rome is a place	e	who make bread.
6	Do you know many people	f	that you can have as pets.

2 Circle the correct answer.

1 Did you see the film ___ was on television at eleven o'clock last night?

   a which   b what   c where

2 I don't know the doctor ___ son is in my class.

   a who   b whose   c which

3 I once went to a restaurant ___ they only make pizza.

   a which   b where   c when

4 My friend Denise is the person ___ clothes I borrow.

   a who   b which   c whose

5 Where's the person ___ sold you this bike?

   a whose   b –   c who

6 Have you found the book ___ you lost yesterday?

   a that   b what   c where

7 I've never met the girl ___ wrote this essay.

   a who   b whose   c who's

8 Leo's the person ___ I have invited to my house on Saturday.

   a –   b which   c whose

3 Find the mistakes in the sentences. Then write them correctly.

1 My parents, <u>which</u> live in central London, would love to live in the country.

   <u>My parents, who live in central London, would love to live in the country.</u>

2 Where's the pair of jeans what you were wearing yesterday?

   _____

3 My aunt and uncle who live in the USA, are coming to stay with us.

   _____

4 Have you been to the new clothes shop where is next to the bank?

   _____

5 Shakespeare is a writer which plays I enjoy watching on stage.

   _____

6 The Acropolis, that is a popular tourist attraction, is in Athens.

   _____

7 He is an actor, has got lovely eyes.

   _____

8 Do you know a person can fix my computer?

   _____

4 **Circle the correct answer.**

1 Jarek loves ___ in the summer.
   (a) windsurfing   b the windsurfing   c to windsurfing

2 I forgot ___ the plants this morning.
   a watered   b watering   c to water

3 I imagine ___ on the moon would be extremely strange!
   a to live   b being lived   c living

4 Do you mind ___ me your laptop for the weekend?
   a lending   b to lend   c to lending

5 I can't persuade Mum ___ me come to the party this evening.
   a to let   b let   c letting

6 Dana never goes anywhere without ___ her favourite top.
   a she puts on   b putting on   c to put on

7 I hate ___ you, but can you give me some more money?
   a be asking   b asking   c to asking

8 ___ is an excellent form of exercise.
   a To swim   b The swimming   c Swimming

5 **Complete the sentences with the gerund or the infinitive.**

1 He admitted _____lying_____ (lie) to his mum.

2 Where did you learn _____ (play) tennis so well?

3 If you can't get your computer to work, try _____ it _____ (turn off) for a few seconds.

4 Don't forget _____ (feed) the cats before you go out this evening.

5 Did you finish _____ (tidy) your room yesterday?

6 He isn't very good at _____ (use) a camera.

7 I'm so happy _____ (see) you again after so long!

8 It was a long journey, so we stopped _____ (get) something to eat on the way.

6 **Find the mistakes in the sentences. Then write them correctly.**

1 In the winter she usually goes to ski.
   In the winter she usually goes skiing.

2 I hope seeing you during the weekend.
   _____

3 It's just too hot for going out today.
   _____

4 Did you manage find your purse?
   _____

5 Is the pizza enough cool to eat yet?
   _____

6 Do you regret to do your homework while you were tired?
   _____

7 Do you remember to meet those nice people last year?
   _____

8 I often spend time to go on the internet.
   _____

7 **Complete the sentences with the verbs from the box. Use the causative.**

| check | ~~not cut~~ | dye | fix | inspect | make | paint | test |

1 I _____ haven't had my hair cut _____ for ages. (my hair)

2 At the border between the two countries, everyone
   _____ . (their passports)

3 He _____ by his dad when I saw him. (his bike)

4 She _____ for her party next Saturday. (a special dress)

5 I _____ once a year. (my eyes)

6 I _____ this weekend. (my bedroom)

7 An actor I saw on TV _____ green! (her hair)

8 I _____ at the dentist's tomorrow. (my teeth)

8 **Complete the sentences by writing one word in each gap.**

1 She _____ has _____ her hair dyed a different colour every year.

2 Is your Dad _____ the car washed this weekend?

3 My brother has _____ the walls of his room painted blue.

4 She had all her carpets _____ after the party.

5 Luckily, we had _____ our TV repaired by the time the match started.

6 My sister _____ an appointment made for the dentist's.

7 I _____ going to have my hair cut tomorrow.

8 He _____ having all the books delivered to our school tomorrow.

9 **Write questions using the causative. Use the past simple.**

1 Mum / the new sofa / deliver / yesterday / ?
   Did Mum have the new sofa delivered yesterday?

2 you / your old computer / fix / last month / ?
   _____

3 the school / a new gym / build / last year / ?
   _____

4 they / their party / organise / by Peng / ?
   _____

5 the boys / their photo / take / at the studio / ?
   _____

6 your grandmother / her flat / paint / last week / ?
   _____

7 she / the books / send / to her / from the USA / ?
   _____
   _____

8 he / his homework / check / by the new teacher / ?
   _____
   _____

10 Complete the sentences with the phrases from the box. There may be more than one possible answer.

~~as~~   because   because of   due to   in case   in order to   the reason why   to

1 _____As_____ they had so much food, they decided to invite some friends.

2 _____ his broken leg, he couldn't play football.

3 _____ they wanted to go to the park was that it was a beautiful day.

4 He went to the shop _____ buy some envelopes.

5 _____ keep fit, she went to the gym three times a week.

6 My friends couldn't come to the party _____ they had visitors.

7 Take some games with you _____ you get bored.

8 _____ the extreme heat, we jumped into the swimming pool.

11 Complete the sentences with the words from the box. There may be more than one possible answer.

although   but   even though   however   so (x2)   such   ~~whereas~~

1 _____Whereas_____ I prefer holidays by the sea, my parents prefer mountain holidays.

2 _____ she was feeling ill, she still went to school.

3 A lot of them wanted to go on the school trip, _____ the school booked three coaches.

4 It was _____ a hot day that all we wanted to do was to swim in the sea.

5 She studied hard all day and felt tired. _____ , she still went out later with her friends.

6 The teacher spoke _____ quickly I couldn't understand him.

7 My brother wanted the cheese pizza, _____ Mum bought him a salad.

8 _____ she was not working very hard, she managed to pass all her exams!

12 Circle the correct answer.

1 I didn't know that there were ___ people in this city!

  a such a lot   (b) so many   c so much

2 In spite of ___ a bad headache, she still went to school.

  a to have   b having   c she had

3 The journey was difficult because of the rain. ___ , we got there safely.

  a Although   b Whereas   c However

4 Where did you find ___ nice jacket?

  a such a   b so   c such

5 They didn't pay the bill and, ___ , they had the electricity cut off.

  a as a result   b the reason   c even though

6 It was Pete's birthday, ___ he decided to take some friends to the cinema.

  a so that   b while   c so

7 ___ his bad behaviour, the head teacher had to have a word with him.

  a Since   b Because of   c Due

8 We should eat now in case we ___ anything to eat on the way.

  a don't find   b find   c won't find

1 **Complete the words.**

1   Satomi likes speaking to people. She's a t <u>a</u> <u>l</u> <u>k</u> <u>a</u> <u>t</u> <u>i</u> <u>v</u> <u>e</u> person.

2   Our teacher always arrives at seven o'clock. He's very r __ __ __ __ __ __ __ .

3   You can trust an h __ __ __ __ __ friend.

4   Katya loves giving presents to others. She's g __ __ __ __ __ __ __ .

5   Carlos loves clothes. He's really f __ __ __ __ __ __ __ __ __ .

6   Adam will be a great artist one day. He's extremely t __ __ __ __ __ __ __ .

7   My uncle is a m __ __ __ __ __-__ __ __ __ man, but he still enjoys playing football.

8   Teachers should be p __ __ __ __ __ __ .

2 **Read Alina's description of a person she admires. Write *T* for true and *F* for false.**

I've chosen to write about my aunt Erica. I've known her since I was a little girl. She's the best vet in my neighbourhood and I think she's a very special person.

Aunt Erica is in her early forties. She's quite fashionable and she's usually well dressed. She's always been a very shy person, so she's not very talkative. She's one of the most caring people I've ever met and that's why she's always very busy. Everyone goes to her when their pets are ill.

She doesn't have very much free time as she also looks after animals that haven't got homes. Most people in our area know Erica, so if they find an animal in the street, they phone her and take it to her. She can't keep all the pets that people bring, but she takes care of them until she finds a home for them. She's very patient with animals and she's also extremely honest.

I admire Erica most because she shows that she really cares about animals. She doesn't only help them because it's her job.

1   Erica works in Alina's neighbourhood.   <u>T</u>

2   Alina's aunt doesn't talk a lot.   __

3   People trust Erica with their pets.   __

4   Erica has got lots of free time.   __

5   Erica keeps all the pets she is given.   __

6   Erica helps animals because she loves them.   __

3 **Read again. In which paragraph does Alina say**

1   what the person does that she admires?   _3_
2   how old the person is and what she looks like?   ___
3   who she's chosen to write about?   ___
4   why she admires the person most?   ___
5   how long she's known her?   ___
6   what the person is like?   ___

4 **Complete Alina's writing plan.**

Paragraph 1: _say who I've chosen to write about, how long I've known her and what I think of her_

Paragraph 2: _____

Paragraph 3: _____

Paragraph 4: _____

5 **Alina used the words from the box in her description. Find the words and underline them. Answer the questions.**

> ~~and~~   as   because   but   so

Which word(s) do we use

1   to add information?   _____and_____
2   to show contrast?   _____
3   to give reasons?   _____ and _____
4   to show a result?   _____

6 **Read another description. Circle the correct words to complete the description.**

I've chosen to write about Ed, my basketball coach. He's been my coach for two years [1] (and) / but he's a really special person.

Ed is in his mid-twenties and he's very well built. He usually dresses casually [2] because / so he doesn't need to wear special clothes to work. He's a sociable person [3] and / as he's very talkative with everyone in our basketball club.

Ed is a very patient person, [4] but / so he doesn't expect us to be excellent players immediately. He says we could do really well [5] as / but we all work hard. I wasn't very good at basketball when I joined the club, [6] because / but Ed taught me to play well. He makes us train a lot, [7] so / but we haven't got time to be lazy.

I admire Ed most [8] because / and he's patient. He has helped me and my friends to become a great team. He's a caring person and we all love him.

Now it's your turn!

7 **Use Alina's writing plan to make notes for your description of a person you admire.**

My writing plan notes
Paragraph 1: _____
Paragraph 2: _____
Paragraph 3: _____
Paragraph 4: _____

8 **Now use your writing plan notes to write a description of a person you admire. Write in your notebook.**

1 **Complete the crossword.**

Across

3 This paper shows that you've passed a special exam.

6 You do sports in this lesson.

8 You must get a good one to pass your exam.

9 I have to do this to be ready for my maths test.

10 This is a group of lessons on a subject.

Down

1 Your hands get dirty making things in this lesson.

2 Students have to stay at school late for this when they behave badly.

4 This is one of the science subjects.

5 This is a tasty subject!

7 You visit different places with your teachers when you go on one of these.

2 **Read Robert's email about a course he is doing. Answer the questions.**

From: Robert   **To:** Sebastian   **Subject:** my French course

Dear Sebastian,

I'm writing to you from a village in France where I'm doing a summer course in French. We've got a very friendly teacher whose lessons are really interesting.

The course is at a small school which is in a beautiful part of the countryside. It's got small classrooms, which are clean and bright, and there are really nice gardens all around. The food's great too! It's made by the students on the cookery course.

We have lessons every morning from Monday to Friday. Then we go on trips to different places in the area, where we have picnics and speak to the local people. In the evening, we sometimes play games and we do revision for our final exam, which is on Friday morning.

I'm travelling back on Sunday morning with a friend called Kostas, who I've spent the week with here. We're looking forward to getting our certificates before we leave.

See you soon,

Robert

1 Why is Robert in France?   He's doing a summer course in French.

2 What are the lessons like?   _____

3 Where is the school?   _____

4 When does Robert have lessons?   _____

5 What two things does Robert do in the evenings?   _____

6 Who is Robert travelling home with?   _____

3 **Read again. In which paragraph does Robert say**

1 when he'll be back and who he is travelling with? <u>4</u>

2 where he is, what he is doing and what his teacher is like? ___

3 what the school is like? ___

4 what he's looking forward to? ___

5 what they do every day? ___

6 where the place is and what it's like? ___

4 **Complete Robert's writing plan.**

Greeting:	<u>Dear Sebastian,</u> _____
Paragraph 1:	_____
Paragraph 2:	_____
Paragraph 3:	_____
Paragraph 4:	_____
Ending:	_____
Sign off:	_____

5 **Robert used the words from the box in his email. Find the words and underline them. Then answer the questions.**

> where   which   ~~who~~   whose

Which word(s) do we use

1 to refer to a person? <u>who</u>

2 to refer to a place? _____

3 to refer to something? _____

4 to show that something belongs to a person or place? _____

6 **Read another email. Complete the email with *where, which, who* or *whose*.**

From: Sophie   **To:** Jana   **Subject:** my German course

Dear Jana,

I'm writing to you from a town in Germany ¹_____where_____ I'm on a course learning German.
I've got a very funny teacher ²_____ lessons are really enjoyable.

The course is at a school ³_____ is in the town centre. It's a huge building and it's got
a fantastic library. There are restaurants, cafés and cinemas nearby, so it's very noisy!

We have lessons in the morning three times a week. In the afternoon, we usually go to the park,
⁴_____ we play football or tennis or go for walks. In the evening, we go to a local restaurant,
⁵_____ has got great food!

I'm flying back in two weeks with my cousin Felipe, ⁶_____ is doing the same course as me.
We're both looking forward to getting our certificates at the end of the course.

See you soon,

Sophie

Now it's your turn!

7 **Imagine you are at a language school in another country. Use Robert's writing plan to make notes for your email to a friend.**

My writing plan notes

Greeting: _____

Paragraph 1:   _____

Paragraph 2:   _____

Paragraph 3:   _____

Paragraph 4:   _____

Ending: _____

Sign off: _____

8 **Now use your writing plan notes to write an email to a friend about the language school. Write in your notebook.**

1 **Read what the newspapers say about the new TV programmes. Complete the words.**

1   A great c _o_ _m_ _e_ _d_ _y_ ! It made us laugh a lot!

2   It's the best s ___ ___ ___ o ___ ___ ___ ___ in the world.

3   A new r ___ ___ ___ ___ ___ ___ s ___ ___ ___ that shows the lives of different celebrities at home.

4   The p ___ ___ ___ is a bit strange, but the film is really good!

5   A new police d ___ ___ ___ ___ about a strange detective who solves a mystery.

6   Most of the film is predictable, but the end is really s ___ ___ ___ ___ ___ ___ ___ ___ ___ .

7   A different kind of s ___ ___ ___ ___ ___ ___ -f ___ ___ ___ ___ ___ ___ film that isn't about space.

8   Thanks to the brilliant c ___ ___ ___ of new actors, this adventure film is great!

2 **Read Viviana's film review and answer the questions.**

Summer Surprise

starring Emma Fisher and Kate Wyles

The film

Summer Surprise is a comedy about two students who are travelling after they've graduated from university. Their last stop is a small fishing village in southern Italy, where most of the film is set.

The story

The stars of the film, Emma Fisher and Kate Wyles, team up with two new actors, Nancy Stokes and Elena Lombardi. During a trip around Europe, Jane and Katie (Wyles and Stokes) decide to stay in Italy for the summer. They grow to love the village and make some new friends (Fisher and Lombardi, who play the Italians). Six months later, summer is over and the two girls are still enjoying pizza and cappuccino in the village square.

The good and the bad

Thanks to the cast, the film is a great success. There are some very funny scenes, which make the film even more entertaining. The plot is easy to follow but quite predictable, just like the ending.

My advice

If you want to relax at the cinema and have a good laugh, go and watch this film. Don't expect a 'summer surprise' though. There aren't any surprises in this film.

1   What kind of film is *Summer Surprise*?   _____ a comedy _____
2   Which two main actors star in the film?   _____
3   How long do the girls plan to stay in Italy?   _____
4   Why do the girls end up staying?   _____
5   Why is the film a great success?   _____
6   What does Viviana say about the ending?   _____

3 **Read again. In which paragraph does Viviana say**

1   whether she thinks the film is worth watching?   _4_

2   who stars in the film?   ___

3   what the plot is?   ___

4   what type of film it is?   ___

5   where it is set?   ___

6   what is good or bad about the film?   ___

4 **Complete Viviana's writing plan.**

Title: _Summer Surprise_ _____

Paragraph 1: _____

Paragraph 2: _____

Paragraph 3: _____

Paragraph 4: _____

5 **Viviana used the subheadings below so the reader knows what information will be in each paragraph. Read the subheadings.**

Paragraph 1:   The film

Paragraph 2:   The story

Paragraph 3:   The good and the bad

Paragraph 4:   My advice

Subheadings can also be questions. Which paragraphs match these new subheadings?

1   What's the plot?   _2_

2   What's good and what's bad?   ___

3   Is it worth seeing?   ___

4   What is the film?   ___

6 Read another review about the new film *Shake*. The paragraphs from the review are in the wrong order. Number the paragraphs in order. Then write the correct questions from Exercise 5 as subheadings.

Shake

Starring Kamil Karr and Marina Alloatti

1 ___ Rob (Karr) and his sister Tina (Alloatti) are riding their bike one evening when they see a bright light coming from the aeroplane. Every time they get closer to the plane, the light disappears. They take their friends to see this strange light, and they all decide that the plane is a time machine and that somebody is using it to travel through time.

2 ___ It's not the best science-fiction film, but if you enjoy films about time travel and you don't have anything better to do, go and see the film.

3 ___ The group of young actors is brilliant, but the plot suddenly disappears, just like the bright light, and the ending isn't at all surprising.

 What is the film?

4 _1_ *Shake* is a science-fiction film about two children who find an old aeroplane in the middle of a field, where most of the film is set. They believe that something strange is happening in the plane.

Now it's your turn!

7 Use Viviana's writing plan to make notes for your film review.

My writing plan notes

Title: _____

Paragraph 1: _____

Paragraph 2: _____

Paragraph 3: _____

Paragraph 4: _____

8 Now use your writing plan notes to write a film review. Write in your notebook.

1 Complete the crossword.

Across

2 All football players dream of playing in the _____ Cup.

5 Which country won the most gold medals in the last Olympic _____ ?

7 There'll be lots of famous actors at the film _____ .

8 Would you like to _____ in a special event?

9 All the runners were wearing _____ .

10 How many people will run in the London _____ this year?

Down

1 The bands raised a lot of money for charity at the _____ .

3 The evening ended with a fantastic fireworks _____ .

4 We saw some wonderful costumes in the _____ procession.

6 _____ is another word for a famous person.

2 Read Anton's narrative about a special event. Write *T* for true and *F* for false.

Last year, my family and I went to Venice, one of the most amazing places I've ever visited. In February every year, thousands of visitors from all over the world travel there to take part in the spectacular carnival.

As soon as we arrived at our hotel, we put on our costumes and set out on our adventure. As we walked through the busy streets, we couldn't believe our eyes! The tiny streets and main square were full of people wearing amazing costumes! We noticed bands playing different kinds of music and people singing and dancing all around us. The atmosphere was incredible. Dad was taking some pictures, and suddenly a tall man came up to us and asked if he could take our picture. We were all surprised and wondered why he wanted a photo of us. Dad carried on talking to him for a while, then said that we had to go and have lunch. At that moment, the man took off his mask and told us that we had three of the best costumes he had seen that day. He invited us to take part in the final fancy-dress competition.

Later on, we had lunch in one of the local restaurants. Then we decided to go back and relax at our hotel. We were happy and very excited. We were looking forward to the evening and we didn't want to be too tired.

The celebration that night was out of this world! There were dancers, acrobats and actors performing in a beautiful outdoor theatre. We went on stage with thirty other people in fancy dress so that the best costume could be chosen. In the end, we didn't win a prize, but this was one of the most exciting days of my life!

1 The carnival in Venice takes place once a year. T

2 Anton and his parents walked around Venice in their own clothes. ___

3 The streets were busy and noisy. ___

4 Anton's dad wanted to take a picture of a tall man. ___

5 Anton and his family relaxed in a local restaurant. ___

6 Anton's family won a prize for their costumes. ___

3 **Read again. In which paragraph does Anton say**

1   what they did when they arrived at their hotel?   _2_

2   what happened finally?   ___

3   where he visited?   ___

4   when he went?   ___

5   who he went with?   ___

6   what they did before they went out in the evening?   ___

7   what he saw and heard around him?   ___

4 **Complete Anton's writing plan.**

Paragraph 1:   say where I visited, when I went and who I went with

Paragraph 2:   _____

Paragraph 3:   _____

Paragraph 4:   _____

5 **Anton used the phrasal verbs below in his narrative. Find the phrasal verbs and underline them. Then match them with their meaning.**

1   carry on   a   approach
2   come up to   b   continue
3   put on   c   participate in
4   set out   d   dress in something
5   take part in   e   remove
6   take off   f   start a journey

6 Read another narrative about a special event. Complete it with the phrasal verbs from Exercise 5 in the correct form.

A month ago, I went to visit my cousin in Lewes, east Sussex, where Guy Fawkes Night is a huge tradition. In Lewes, they don't just put the Guy on the bonfire and enjoy fireworks. People wear fancy-dress costumes and walk around the streets. I couldn't wait to ¹ ___take part in___ this amazing celebration.

As soon as I arrived at my cousin's house, we ² _____ our fancy-dress costumes and ³ _____ on our walk to the town centre. The atmosphere was great and some of the costumes spectacular. While we were walking along the street, a man in an unusual costume ⁴ _____ us and started talking. I was a bit scared, so I ⁵ _____ walking. Suddenly, he jumped in front of me and ⁶ _____ his mask. At that moment, I realised that it was my uncle Joe. I couldn't believe my eyes!

Later on, we walked along the crowded streets, full of people in magnificent costumes. Then we went to watch a fancy-dress competition at the town hall, where they picked the best costume. Uncle Joe won second prize for his costume and we were all proud of him. It was an amazing event and we had a very good time.

In the end, we went outside and watched a fantastic fireworks display which was out of this world. This was one of the most exciting nights of my life!

Now it's your turn!

7 Imagine you have taken part in a special event. Use Anton's writing plan to make notes for your narrative describing it.

My writing plan notes

Paragraph 1: _____

Paragraph 2: _____

Paragraph 3: _____

Paragraph 4: _____

8 Now use your writing plan notes to write a narrative about a special event. Write in your notebook.

1 **Match the words with the descriptions.**

1	rainforest	a	An important area of countryside protected by the government.
2	glacier	b	A mountain that can erupt with fire, smoke and lava.
3	volcano	c	Very dry land where it does not rain very often.
4	desert	d	The native wild animals of a region.
5	peak	e	A very large expanse of sea.
6	ocean	f	The pointed top or the highest point of a mountain.
7	national park	g	A tropical forest with a heavy rainfall.
8	wildlife	h	A slow moving river of ice.

2 **Read Duncan's article about the Cairngorms National Park. Answer the questions.**

A trip to natural relaxation

Are you looking for a peaceful break in a beautiful setting? If you are, come and visit the Cairngorms National Park, which is Britain's largest national park. It is located in the north of Scotland and covers an area of 3,800 square kilometres.

The park is amazing. There are huge mountain peaks, which are actually extinct volcanoes, together with magnificent rivers, calm lakes and lovely plants. While you're walking around, you'll see animals and birds everywhere.

At the park, there are plenty of activities too. You can enjoy mountain biking, climbing or canoeing in all seasons in this wonderful environment. If you want something more relaxing, you can go on a guided walk in the forests, where you'll learn about the beautiful plants and animals. People who are interested in birds can enjoy bird watching and, if you are lucky, you might even see a golden eagle. Winter visitors can also go skiing.

Every year, thousands of visitors enjoy these peaceful surroundings. Why don't you join them?

1	Where is the national park?	in the north of Scotland
2	What size is the park?	_____
3	What can you see when you walk around the park?	_____
4	What activities can you enjoy at any time of the year?	_____
5	What can you do if you like birds?	_____
6	What winter sport can you do?	_____

3 **Read again. In which paragraph does Duncan**

1 say what activities you can do there? _3_

2 say what you can see? ___ , ___

3 say what the area is like? ___

4 say where the park is? ___

5 ask a question? ___ , ___

4 **Complete Duncan's writing plan.**

Title:	A trip to natural relaxation
Paragraph 1:	
Paragraph 2:	
Paragraph 3:	
Paragraph 4:	

5 **Read the steps Duncan used to write his article. Then match the phrases and sentences with the steps.**

Steps	What Duncan wrote
1 Use a title that will make readers want to read on.	A trip to natural relaxation
2 Ask a question to make the introduction more interesting.	Are you looking for a peaceful break in a natural setting?
3 Tell the readers what they can see there.	While you're walking around …
4 Tell the readers about the activities available.	At the park, there are plenty of activities …
5 Give the readers a choice.	If you want something more relaxing …
6 End your article in a way that will make the readers want to know more.	Why don't you join them?

1 If you want some action … _4_

2 Would you like to enjoy an adventure by the Pacific Ocean? ___

3 What are you waiting for? ___

4 While you explore this area … ___

5 Adventure in a natural environment ___

6 For something more relaxing … ___

6 Read another article about the Pacific Rim National Park. Complete the article with the phrases and sentences from Exercise 5.

1 _____Adventure in a natural environment_____

2 _____
_____

If so, visit the Pacific Rim National Park, located in British Columbia, Canada.

This huge national park has got lovely beaches together with thick rainforests and mountains. There are lakes and long rivers, which used to be glaciers, everywhere.

3 _____ ,

you'll see different kinds of birds such as eagles, and mammals such as deer, wolves and bears, and the ocean is full of many kinds of whales and fish.

4 _____ ,

you can try surfing, diving, kayaking or canoeing.

5 _____ ,

you can go bird watching or just enjoy a long walk along the beach and admire the shells. You might be lucky enough to see a whale too.

There's so much to discover and enjoy.

6 _____

Now it's your turn!

7 Use Duncan's writing plan to make notes for your article about a national park in your country.

> **My writing plan notes**
>
> Title: _____
>
> Paragraph 1: _____
>
> Paragraph 2: _____
>
> Paragraph 3: _____
>
> Paragraph 4: _____

8 Now use your writing plan notes to write an article about a national park. Write in your notebook.

1 Complete the table with the words from the box to show where you can buy them.

biscuits	bread	cake	cucumber	dress	earrings	necklace	pear	pie
potatoes	ring	skirt	tights	trousers	watch	watermelon		

Baker's	Clothes shop	Greengrocer's	Jeweller's
biscuits			

2 Ayo wrote a story which ends with the words *'It was the most embarrassing day of my life!'* Read his story and write *T* for true and *F* for false.

Three weeks ago, we got a leaflet in the post about a new department store in our town. There was a special offer with about 30% off everything in the shop. I kept the leaflet, and yesterday Mum and I decided to go.

When we got to the department store, we couldn't believe how big it was. I was so excited. Mum saw a dress for 40€, I found a pair of shoes for the same price and we got three pairs of socks for Dad, which were 2€ a pair on the leaflet. We chose a leather handbag for my aunt's birthday. The quality was great and the price was high, but we thought it would be a bargain with the discount.

Mum and I had filled up our basket and we went to pay. We were really happy with how much we'd bought for the low price we would pay. Well, that's what we thought.

In the end, the bill came to 150€! I told Mum not to worry and I showed the leaflet to the shop assistant with the discounts on everything we had bought. She pointed to the top, where 'Shop this week' was written. I got the leaflet three weeks ago! I didn't know what to do. Mum didn't want to pay more than 100€. It was the most embarrassing day of my life!

1	Ayo went shopping three weeks ago.	F
2	Ayo's shoes cost 40€.	___
3	The leaflet mentioned socks at 2€ a pair.	___
4	The handbag was expensive without the discount.	___
5	Ayo's mum was happy to pay 150€ for their shopping.	___
6	The shop assistant gave Ayo the discount when he showed her the leaflet.	___

3 **Read again. In which paragraph does Ayo say**

1   what happened in the end?   <u>4</u>

2   when and how the whole story started?   ___

3   what the shop was like and what they wanted to buy?   ___

4   what happened when they went to pay?   ___

5   how they felt when they had filled their basket?   ___

4 **Complete Ayo's writing plan.**

Paragraph 1: <u>say when and how the whole story started</u> _____

Paragraph 2: _____

Paragraph 3: _____

Paragraph 4: _____

5 **Before Ayo wrote his story, he asked himself some questions to help him make his plan. Read the information below.**

Who is the main character?

What is the story about?

When did it happen?

Where did it happen?

How did the people feel at the beginning of the story?

How did the story develop?

Why was it the most embarrassing day of his life?

Before you start writing a story, you should

• think of a good idea.

• think about who the main character is, when the story took place and where it took place.

• think about a good ending that fits in with the set phrase.

When you're writing a story, you should

• introduce the idea at the beginning of each paragraph with a topic sentence and then develop the idea, e.g. **Three weeks ago, we got a leaflet in the post about a new department store in our town.** *There was a special offer with about 30% off everything in the shop.*

   Mum and I had filled up our basket and we went to pay. *We were really happy with how much we'd bought for the low price we would pay.*

   In the end, the bill came to 150€! *I told Mum not to worry and I showed the leaflet to the shop assistant with the discounts on everything we had bought.*

• make sure the paragraphs are in a logical order.

• end the story using the set phrase given without changing it.

Story: writing about a shopping experience

6 Read another a story, which ends with the words *'It was the most disappointing day of my life!'* Complete it with the sentences from the box.

> My friends told me that in that shop, the prices were too high and that the quality wasn't any better.
>
> Finally, the night of the school dance arrived.
>
> I didn't like the idea of shopping from a catalogue though.
>
> ~~A few months ago, my friends and I wanted to find something to wear to the school dance.~~
>
> When I walked in, I couldn't believe my eyes!
>
> My friend Sally had a catalogue at home, which she did most of her shopping from.

¹ A few months ago, my friends and I wanted to find something to wear to the school dance. We sat at Carrie's house and talked about what we could buy to wear and where we could buy it from. Everyone wanted something that was cheap but good quality.

2 _____
All my friends found something they liked in it and the prices were very low.

3 _____ As the prices weren't high, I thought that the quality would be very bad and I wanted to buy something from the local clothes shop.

4 _____ I didn't believe them, so I went and bought a really expensive dress. I could see that it wasn't anything special, but it was from Marlene's Clothes Shop and everyone knew that.

5 _____ I couldn't wait to show my dress to everyone as I knew they wanted to see the dress I had spent so much money on. 6 _____ Sally and I were wearing exactly the same dress in the same colour. It was the most disappointing day of my life!

Now it's your turn!

7 You are going to write a story about a shopping experience that ends with the words *'It was the most exciting day of my life.'* Use Ayo's writing plan to make notes for your story.

> **My writing plan notes**
>
> Paragraph 1: _____
>
> Paragraph 2: _____
>
> Paragraph 3: _____
>
> Paragraph 4: _____

8 Now use your writing plan notes to write a story. Write in your notebook.

1 **Read the descriptions and complete the words.**

1 An area which is mostly houses.

r e s i d e n t i a l

2 An area or houses on the edge of a city or town.

s __ __ __ __ __

3 The opposite of modern.

o __ __ - __ __ __ __ __ __ __ __

4 A room or building that is big inside.

s __ __ __ __ __ __ __

5 This describes something very small.

t __ __ __

6 A room with too much furniture is this.

c __ __ __ __ __ __

7 Very old furniture which is often expensive.

a __ __ __ __ __ __

8 A shape with four sides of the same size.

s __ __ __ __ __

2 **Read Pam's description of her home. Write T for true and F for false.**

My home

My home is in a place called Pagrati, which is a suburb of Athens. I've been living here for ten years and I like this area very much. It's a quiet residential area, which has got a big park and a few shops on the main road nearby.

I live in a flat on the third floor of a small building. When you go in the front door there's a spacious hall, where we've got a lovely little antique Italian glass table and two comfortable red chairs. Then there's a door to a living room with a modern fireplace and a large kitchen with beautiful, big wooden cupboards. At the back, there are two bedrooms and a bathroom.

What I like most about my house is my bedroom. I've just decorated it and I've bought a new square, green rug, which goes well with my bright, yellow curtains. It's a quiet room and I love the view of the park at the back of the building.

1 Pam doesn't live in the city centre. T

2 There are no shops near the house. __

3 Pam lives in a small house. __

4 The hall in Pam's flat is quite small. __

5 The fireplace looks old. __

6 Pam can see the park from her bedroom. __

3 **Read again. In which paragraph does Pam say**

1   what she likes most about her home?   _3_

2   what area she lives in?   —

3   what the area is like?   —

4   what her home is like?   —

5   how long she's been living there?   —

4 **Complete Pam's writing plan.**

Title: _My home_ _____

Paragraph 1:   _____

Paragraph 2:   _____

Paragraph 3:   _____

5 **Pam used the words below in her description. Find the words and underline them.**
Then answer the questions.

cupboards   rug   table

What adjectives does Pam use to describe

1   the table? _____

2   the cupboards? _____

3   the rug? _____

In English, adjectives must be used in the right order. The table below shows the correct order.
Complete the table with the adjectives Pam uses to describe the table, the cupboards and
the rug.

Opinion	Size	Age	Shape	Colour	Origin	Material	Noun
lovely							table
							cupboards
							rug

6 **Read another description of someone's home. Put the adjectives below in the correct order to write the missing phrases.**

1   garden / big / beautiful

2   roses / pink / lovely

3   sofa / modern / blue

4   table / old-fashioned / square

5   chairs / French / antique

6   bookcase / wooden / old

My house

My house is in Sandgate, a suburb of Folkestone. I've been living here since I was born and I love the area. It's a peaceful town by the sea, with a few shops and nice beaches.

I live in a cottage, with a(n)

1 _____ beautiful, big garden _____ full of

2 _____ . My house isn't very big and it's quite old, but we've just bought

a(n) 3 _____ for the living room. The kitchen is spacious and it's got an old fireplace. By the window, there's

a(n) 4 _____ where we eat our meals and three

5 _____ .

What I like most about my house is our study. It's tiny, but it's got large windows and I can see the garden.

There's a(n) 6 _____ by the door, which used to belong to my grandpa.

Now it's your turn!

7 **Use Pam's writing plan to make notes for your description of your home.**

My writing plan notes

Title: _____

Paragraph 1: _____

Paragraph 2: _____

Paragraph 3: _____

8 **Now use your writing plan notes to write a description of your home. Write in your notebook.**

1 **Complete the crossword.**

¹C

²A ³L

⁴C ⁵R F

É

⁶N

⁷A

⁸B

⁹S

Across

2   There is a bus stop outside the town _____ .

4   Leave your car in the big _____ and you can walk to the shops.

6   My dad buys magazines at the _____ .

7   I go to the bowling _____ every Friday after school.

8   There is a lovely park just one _____ from my house.

9   You can't turn left into Apple Road because it's a one-way _____ .

Down

1   Mum thinks I spend too much time with my friends in the _____ .

3   Stop your car when the traffic _____ are red.

4   The film is on at the _____ on Saturday.

5   There are always lots of cars going round the _____ .

2 **Read Junsu's email about a place which has changed a lot. Answer the questions.**

From: Junsu   **To:** Sam   **Subject:** changes

Hi Sam!

You won't believe where I went at the weekend! I went by bus to my old neighbourhood and I stayed with my aunt Seong. The town has changed so much!

On Saturday, Seong and I went on foot to the town centre. It's easier than going by car, as the town is full of one-way streets now. Do you remember that we used to turn right at the traffic lights and walk along the street to the shops in Court Road? Well, the baker's, chemist's and newsagent's aren't there anymore. There's a huge shopping centre now with a cinema. On the ground floor, there are modern shops and on the first floor, there's a new café, three cinemas and a Greek restaurant. The old town hall has gone too. Now there's a new one next to a big car park.

I don't really like all these changes. There aren't enough places for teenagers to go. I think it needs some sports facilities like a bowling alley and a swimming pool.

I'll send you my photos and you'll see for yourself when I see you on Saturday.

See you then,

Junsu

1   Why did Junsu write about his old neighbourhood?   _because the town has changed so much_

2   Why did Junsu walk to the town centre?   _____

3   Which shops used to be in Court Road?   _____

4   Where are the modern shops in the shopping centre?   _____

5   Which floor is the new café on?   _____

6   What does Junsu think the town needs?   _____

3 **Read again. In which paragraph does Junsu say**

1   what he thinks about the changes and why?   _3_

2   what he did on Saturday?   ___

3   where he went at the weekend and how he got there? ___

4   how the town has changed?   ___

5   when he'll see Sam?   ___

6   where he stayed?   ___

4 **Complete Junsu's writing plan.**

Greeting:	_Hi Sam!_ _____
Paragraph 1:	_____
Paragraph 2:	_____
Paragraph 3:	_____
Paragraph 4:	_____
Ending:	_____
Sign off:	_____

5 **Junsu used the phrases below in his email. Find the phrases and underline them.
Then answer the questions.**

> at the traffic lights   ~~at the weekend~~   by bus   by car   in Court Road
> next to a big car park   on foot   on Saturday   on the first floor
> on the ground floor

Which of the prepositional phrases shows us

1   when something was done? _____at the weekend_____ , _____

2   where something was or where something was done? _____ ,
    _____ , _____ , _____ ,
    _____

3   how someone travelled? _____ , _____ ,
    _____

6 Read another email. Circle the correct words to complete the email.

From: Sabrina   To: Kim   Subject: changes

Hello Kim!

You won't believe where my parents and I went ¹*(at)/ in* the weekend! We went to the town in the Cotswolds where we used to spend our holidays. We went there ² *by / on* car and stayed in a small hotel just outside the town. It has changed so much!

³ *Next to / On* Saturday, we decided to go to the town centre ⁴ *with / on* foot. I saw so many different shops ⁵ *in / by* the High Street. Do you remember the baker's ⁶ *from / next* to the post office? Well, it's now a big café with tables and chairs outside. There's also a roundabout outside the Town Hall and if you turn left ⁷ *at / on* the traffic lights ⁸ *at / by* the end of the High Street, there's a new shopping centre. ⁹ *By / On* the ground floor there are lots of new shops, a large florist's and a French restaurant, which has got very tasty food!

Mum was a bit sad at first because she missed the old shops. Then we had tea ¹⁰ *at / on* the café and we met the old baker, who makes fresh cakes there now. We all agree that the place is more lively than it used to be and it's still very friendly.

I'll show you the pictures when I see you next week!

See you soon,

Sabrina

Now it's your turn!

7 Imagine that you went back to a place where you used to go which has changed a lot. Use Junsu's writing plan to make notes for your email to a friend.

My writing plan notes

Greeting: _____

Paragraph 1: _____

Paragraph 2: _____

Paragraph 3: _____

Ending: _____

Sign off: _____

8 Now use your writing plan notes to write an email to a friend about the place. Write in your notebook.

1 **Complete the table with the words from the box.**

> ~~beach~~   bed and breakfast   by plane   by ship   by train   cabin   chalet
> cruise   flight   full board   half board   hotel   safari   self-catering
> skiing   villa

Type of holiday	Transport	Accommodation
beach		

2 **Read Teresa's narrative about a journey. Write *T* for true and *F* for false.**

A journey to remember

Last year, my family and I went to Greece. The day we left our house, I was so excited! Although it was cold and wet at home, I put on my summer clothes. We got into the taxi and we were driven to the airport.

Our flight left at nine in the morning and got to Athens at two in the afternoon. We had woken up early and I was very tired. As a result, I slept during the whole flight and I missed lunch! When we arrived, we were taken to the port to catch the boat to the island of Paros.

At the port, it was very windy and the boat didn't leave straightaway. Even though I had been on a boat before, I took some sweets with me, just in case I didn't feel well. One hour later, the boat left. My brother wanted to go outside. Although I felt ill, I agreed to go with him. As soon as I went outside, I felt terrible and I sat down. I couldn't find my sweets anywhere! I could see big waves and that's the last thing I remembered.

A few minutes later, I was lying down inside a cabin. My brother was laughing. I felt hungry as I hadn't eaten all day, so Dad got me a sandwich. After I had eaten, I felt a lot better. However, I decided to stay inside for the rest of the journey!

1	Teresa went to Greece two years ago.	F
2	They took their family car to the airport.	___
3	Teresa and her family went to Paros by plane.	___
4	It was the first time Teresa had been on a boat.	___
5	Teresa felt ill when she went outside with her brother.	___
6	After Teresa had eaten, she went outside again.	___

3 **Read again. In which paragraph does Teresa talk about**

1   her journey by plane?   _2_

2   what happened just before and after the boat left the port?   ___

3   how she felt when she left home?   ___

4   when she travelled, who she was travelling with and where to? ___

5   what happened in the end?   ___

6   how the weather was when they set off from home?   ___

7   how they got to the airport?   ___

8   what happened when they arrived in Athens?   ___

4 **Complete Teresa's writing plan.**

Title: _A journey to remember_ _____

Paragraph 1: _____

Paragraph 2: _____

Paragraph 3: _____

Paragraph 4: _____

5 **Teresa used the words from the box in her narrative. Find the words and underline them. Then answer the questions.**

> ~~although~~   as a result   even though
>   however   in case   so

Which words are used

1   to show contrast? ____although____ , _____ , _____

2   to show a result? _____ , _____

3   to show a purpose? _____

6   **Read another narrative. Complete the narrative with words from Exercise 5.**

A train journey I'll never forget

Three weeks ago, it was my birthday and my parents wanted to take me somewhere special. On the day, we all woke up early to get the train to London.

¹____Although____ I had been to London many times, I was very excited. We caught the train at Leicester Station. There weren't many people on the train, ²_____ we could sit wherever we wanted and we all sat by the window. The journey passed quite quickly and we soon arrived at Waterloo Station in London. Dad then told us we had to take a train to St Pancras Station and I thought our journey would end there. ³_____, I was in for a surprise!

At St Pancras Station, Mum told us to run ⁴_____ we missed the next train! I began to wonder where we were going!

The train left the station and I started to feel very tired. ⁵_____, I fell asleep. Three hours later, Mum woke me up and I could see lots of colourful buildings. 'Happy birthday!' Mum and Dad shouted. We had arrived at the Disneyland resort in Paris!

Now it's your turn!

7   **Use Teresa's writing plan to make notes for your narrative about a journey you have made.**

My writing plan notes

Title: _____

Paragraph 1:   _____

Paragraph 2:   _____

Paragraph 3:   _____

Paragraph 4:   _____

8   **Now use your writing plan notes to write a narrative about a journey you have made. Write in your notebook.**

1 **Complete the crossword.**

```
            1
            M
                         2
   3
   A  R  C  H  I  T  E  C  T
                              4
                              L
 5
 C

                  6
                  W


 7
 J
```

Across

3   Mike wants to be the _____ who designs the best shopping centre in the world.

5   Jeff is a responsible man who would love to be _____ of a ship.

6   Barry will be happy to be a _____ in the local café.

7   Linda hopes people will read the articles she writes when she's a _____ .

Down

1   Sue's ambition is to work as a car _____ .

2   Winek needs to study chemistry at university to be a _____ .

4   Katya would like to be a _____ in court and help honest people.

5   Laurent cooks well and he wants to be a famous _____ .

2 **Alex wants to become a journalist, but his parents want him to become an architect. He's afraid they may be angry with him and he needs their support. He wrote to his friend, John, asking for advice. Read John's reply and answer the questions.**

From: John   To: Alex   Subject: RE: Advice please

Dear Alex,

I'm sorry to hear that you're having problems. I know how difficult it is when you have to decide what you want to do in the future. It's hard for your parents too. They only want what's best for you.

First of all, I suggest that you sit down and talk to them. Tell them that you've always dreamt of becoming a journalist. Why don't you give them an example of a successful journalist you admire?

If I were you, I'd explain to them exactly why you want to become a journalist, and I'm sure they'll understand. My advice would be to tell them that you'd love to write articles for magazines and newspapers, even stories, and you could show them some of the articles you've already written.

I also think you should tell them that although they are both very good at what they do, everyone is different. Tell them that you respect their work and that you want them to be happy that you already have ambitions for the future. I'm sure they'll agree to support your decision. I really hope my advice is helpful. Please write back soon!

John

1   What does John think is difficult?   _____deciding what to do in the future_____

2   What does John think Alex should do first?   _____

3   What has Alex always dreamt of becoming?   _____

4   What would Alex like to write?   _____

5   What does John ask Alex to do at the end of his email? _____

3   **Read again. In which paragraph does John**

1   tell Alex to explain to his parents what he wants to be?   _2_

2   say what he would do in Alex's position?   ___

3   say he's sorry Alex is having problems?   ___

4   give a final piece of advice?   ___

5   tell Alex his parents want what's best for him?   ___

6   say Alex should explain why he wants to be a journalist?   ___

7   suggest giving an example of someone who does this job?   ___

4   **Complete John's writing plan.**

Greeting:	_Dear Alex,_ _____
Paragraph 1:	_____
Paragraph 2:	_____
Paragraph 3:	_____
Paragraph 4:	_____
Ending:	_____
Sign off:	_____

5   **John used these phrases in his email. Find the phrases and underline them. Then answer the questions.**

> I also think you should ...   I'm sorry to hear that ...   I suggest that ...
> If I were you, I'd ...   ~~I really hope my advice is ...~~   My advice would be ...
> Why don't you ... ?   you could ...

Which phrases are used

1   to end the email? _I really hope my advice is ..._

2   to show understanding? _____

3   to give advice? _____ , _____ ,
_____ , _____ , _____ ,
_____

6 **Read another email. The writer is very upset. She's always dreamt of becoming a scientist, but her teacher has told her that next year she shouldn't study physics and chemistry, as she's much better at languages. She wrote to her friend asking for advice. Read the reply and complete it with the phrases from Exercise 5.**

From: Caroline **To:** Nicky **Subject:** RE: Advice please

Dear Nicky,

¹ ___I'm sorry to hear that___ you're upset and you don't know what to do. It seems that your teacher is only trying to help you choose the subjects that you're best at, without thinking about what your ambitions for the future are.

First of all, ² _____ to make an appointment to talk to the teacher. Tell him just how much you'd love to become a scientist, even though you aren't one of the best students in the physics and chemistry class.

³ _____ explain to him why you are interested in becoming a scientist. Talk about what kind of great scientific discoveries you'd like to make. ⁴ _____ give an example of a famous scientist who didn't get good marks at school?

⁵ _____ you talk to your parents too. ⁶ _____ explain to them that even though you are better at languages, you still do well in science too.

⁷ _____ tell your parents and your teacher that, while you respect their opinions, you've made up your mind to try hard.

⁸ _____ useful.

Please write back soon.

Caroline

Now it's your turn!

7 **Imagine that your friend has sent you an email asking for advice. His ambition is to become a mechanic, as he loves cars and he's good at fixing things, but his father wants him to go to university and study to become a lawyer. Use John's writing plan to make notes for your email giving advice.**

My writing plan notes

Greeting: _____

Paragraph 1: _____

Paragraph 2: _____

Paragraph 3: _____

Paragraph 4: _____

Ending: _____

Sign off: _____

8 **Now use your writing plan notes to write an email giving advice. Write in your notebook.**

Irregular verbs

Infinitive	Past simple	Past participle	Infinitive	Past simple	Past participle
be	was/were	been	lend	lent	lent
beat	beat	beaten	let	let	let
become	became	become	lie	lay	lain
begin	began	begun	light	lit	lit
bite	bit	bitten	lose	lost	lost
blow	blew	blown	make	made	made
break	broke	broken	mean	meant	meant
bring	brought	brought	meet	met	met
build	built	built	pay	paid	paid
burst	burst	burst	put	put	put
buy	bought	bought	read	read	read
catch	caught	caught	ride	rode	ridden
choose	chose	chosen	ring	rang	rung
come	came	come	rise	rose	risen
cost	cost	cost	run	ran	run
cut	cut	cut	say	said	said
deal	dealt	dealt	see	saw	seen
dig	dug	dug	sell	sold	sold
do	did	done	send	sent	sent
draw	drew	drawn	shake	shook	shaken
drink	drank	drunk	shine	shone	shone
drive	drove	driven	shoot	shot	shot
eat	ate	eaten	show	showed	shown
fall	fell	fallen	shut	shut	shut
feed	fed	fed	sing	sang	sung
feel	felt	felt	sit	sat	sat
fight	fought	fought	sleep	slept	slept
find	found	found	speak	spoke	spoken
fly	flew	flown	spend	spent	spent
forbid	forbade	forbidden	spill	spilt	spilt
forget	forgot	forgotten	spread	spread	spread
forgive	forgave	forgiven	spring	sprang	sprung
freeze	froze	frozen	stand	stood	stood
get	got	got	steal	stole	stolen
give	gave	given	stick	stuck	stuck
go	went	gone	sting	stung	stung
grow	grew	grown	sweep	swept	swept
have	had	had	swim	swam	swum
hear	heard	heard	take	took	taken
hide	hid	hidden	teach	taught	taught
hit	hit	hit	tell	told	told
hold	held	held	think	thought	thought
hurt	hurt	hurt	throw	threw	thrown
keep	kept	kept	understand	understood	understood
know	knew	known	wake	woke	woken
lay	laid	laid	wear	wore	worn
lead	led	led	win	won	won
leave	left	left	write	wrote	written

Notes